We Were Seven

A True Story of Fear, Friendship, and Finding in 1980s Luton

Carl Meek

Fuller Vigil

Book Cover by Dissect Designs

First edition 2025

CONTENTS

For WW.

A simple Child,
That lightly draws its breath,
And feels its life in every limb,
What should it know of death?

William Wordsworth, 'We Are Seven'

FOREWORD

I'm sitting in one of these indoor soft play venues, trying to write an introduction for the book. I must have thought it a good place to put pen to paper while my kids are kept entertained. At least I had the sense not to go on the inflatables. Instead, I'm here in the neon-painted café, watching the other adults: parents crawling around in their socks, following their sugar-fuelled toddlers through padded tunnels; wading into pits of bright blue balls, sweaty and ruffled, with their ass-cracks on show. It's here, amongst all this noise and excitement, that I'm having the realization that we never really grow up. Like when I play with my kids at home, I'm transported into those moments of peace and presence where nothing matters. A place of man-boys and women-girls in our old childhoods. Carrying our fears and insecurities on our shoulders as we, Mum and Dad, dance our way through adult life. And everywhere I look now, I see adults as children—kidults—walking the wibbly, wobbly tightrope between youth and maturity. Longing to play. Yearning for the freedom we once had. Wanting to be loved, accepted, praised, and recognized for what we've done. Sulking over unfulfilled potential, missed opportunities, and grasping onto the creations of our young imaginations. Refusing to accept the fact that we are no longer young. Desperately seeking confirmation that we're still alive.

Perhaps we wish for an alternative life to the one we were dealt: a life in which our parents had done things differently. Maybe we wish we had the opportunity to rewrite events and fine-tune our experiences so we could have lived a better life. But if we remember and honour the children we once were, we can accept the adults we've become and praise ourselves for what we've achieved. If we can acknowledge and forgive the mistakes, we can create our own luck. We're still capable at any time in our lives, of inventing ourselves as we go, of doing what we dreamt of when we were kids. We know that the universe will conspire to help us achieve what we want out of life, but our paths are often blocked by fear. Fear of our own wretchedness.

> We fear our highest possibilities. We are generally afraid to become that which we can glimpse in our most perfect moments, under conditions of great courage. We enjoy and even thrill to godlike possibilities we see in ourselves in such peak moments. And yet we simultaneously shiver with weakness, awe, and fear before these very same possibilities.
>
> Abraham Maslo

I came across this passage a long time ago and I realized that many of us live shrouded in a state of almost permanent fear. I know I do. Fear of beginning and ending, and of all the pain and suffering that comes in between. But it's the fear of suffering that is worse than suffering itself.

That fear still lives with me today as a quivery sensation deep inside. The liquid dread of not knowing what's about to come. But I believe one of the things that has allowed me to move forward is that I no longer shy away from it. Thanks to the journey I underwent in writing this book, I am learning to become friends with my fear. I'm becoming accustomed to it rattling in my limbs, hearing its voice hissing through my veins and lurking around the corners of my mind. I wait for it. I sit with it and watch it patiently, like a pervert in a peep show. I used to think this made me tetchy, pessimistic, and cynical. But maybe my lack of apprehension makes me plucky and precocious. I suppose, by virtue of being human, I'm both. And without one, I wouldn't know the other.

In this paradoxical life, we can be whole and still be many things at the same time. Situations and emotions change, blend, and intertwine. It's no use trying to insist otherwise because I am what I am. The light and the dark. Both brave and afraid. A friend, a husband. Man and boy. Father and son.

And that's it. I'm no longer searching for any profound transformation where I emerge from my cocoon fully metamorphosed. It's just an ongoing journey of love and acceptance. A gradual face-to-face realization of who I am and where I'm from. A quest to find my truth.

This book is a collection of memories which I've attempted to weave together to form a picture of lives lived: a mosaic of rough times, dumb decisions, tragedy, trauma, emotional turmoil, struggles, problems, baggage, and things which went wrong. Some big, some small. All important. It tells the drama of ordinary individuals: fallible people trying to do things they thought were important and delivering to the best of their capabilities and circumstances. And in so doing, I have tried to understand how our experiences as children, from the seemingly innocuous to the downright devastating, play a role in shaping everything that follows. And how, if we don't understand the past, we can be frustrated in our present and future.

In relaying anecdotes of parents, siblings, friends, neighbours, I've attempted to bring the truth and keep the past alive; to record the wonders I've seen and honour individuals as I remember them with love and respect. Still, dealing with memories can be a messy business as they are often blurry—I have undoubtedly left things out, misinterpreted information, been petty, and embellished stories—so there are times where I've coloured outside of the lines in my descriptions of events, sometimes by accident, other times by altering some of the details to make the story easier to comprehend and to protect people's privacy. My objective isn't to accuse or asperse but to tell things how I perceived them and, more or less, how they happened.

Where possible, I've attempted to replicate the language of the time and speak from the child's perspective because the age I was when these events took place, the place and its culture, and the era I grew up in are all crucial to understanding how and why they affected me as they did. Naturally, some of this language is not considered 'proper' English, while some of it is, rightly, considered offensive today. Thus, I ask for the reader's patience and understanding.

When kids play, they are creative, innocent, and open. They have the courage to dream and their brains are like damp sponges. They absorb and trust, all while being less aware of the world around them. Children have no idea what's behind or ahead. But they know stuff. Like I always knew I was going to write this. I'm not talking about superstition or seeing into the future. It's just an innate ability to be still and look closely at the things around you, to penetrate the soul and find a connection.

Some people meditate to find themselves. My wife likes running marathons. Me? I suppose I'm a writer now.

Part 1

The Before

Chapter 1
Little Daryl's Dead

What if I should discover that the poorest of the beggars and the most impudent of offenders are all within me, and that I stand in need of the alms of my own kindness; that I myself am the enemy who must be loved—what then?

Carl Jung

It was the end of 1986. The week after Christmas. I remember because I'd seen that old crow Maggie Thatcher on the telly. She was saying 1987 was going to be a good year and was rabbiting on about money and banks. But I didn't know about any of that stuff, so my attention was focused elsewhere. Dressed in my blue paisley pyjamas, I was sitting on the patched-up pale green sofa, facing the hole in the wall that was meant to be a kind of serving hatch to pass things through from the kitchen. The flat funky aroma of stale wine cut through the air. The offending bottle and glasses were huddled around a fully loaded brass ashtray which was parked on the floor nearby. Mum and Martin were standing toe to toe on the other side of the hatch, talking quietly and quickly, half arguing. Martin looked nervously toward me. He was silent for a moment, then belched it right out of his mouth:

'Little Daryl's dead.'

Little Daryl was a kid who lived on our block. I don't know why we called him Little Daryl: he wasn't all that little, and there weren't any bigger Daryls we could've compared him to. Me and Little Daryl played out every day, on beat-up BMXs with buckled wheels, or bombing up and down the street on our tiptoes. Sometimes, when it was hot, we'd just sit by the side of the road, picking away at the gooey tarmac with a lolly stick. Other times, we leaned planks of wood against the wall in the alley and took turns kicking them while making karate noises. We played in my back garden, too, building hideouts amongst all the weeds and brambles. And there was this shady patch down behind the shed where my mum had her rockery. She grew all sorts of plants there, even some that you could eat, like strawberries and chives and mint. We called it the octopus's garden. And she had this gooseberry bush down there, too, but if you ate one of those sour gooseberries, it would make your mouth pucker up like a cat's bum. There were even some leafy rhubarb stalks poking out of the ground. One time, when me and Daryl were playing there, my mum came out and she cut off some of those pinky-green rhubarbs, and she handed us a little stick each. And then she went back into the house and fetched us a cup of sugar to dip the crunchy rhubarb in. Weird but nice.

After hearing what Martin said about Little Daryl, I just stared at the spider plant that was sitting slumped in the corner by the window. I don't think I could've moved off the sofa even if I'd wanted to. I was having this weird wobbly sensation as if everything was tumbling down, like a physical expression of the slow-motion explosions at the beginning of *The A-Team*. I imagined it was how King Louie must've felt in *The Jungle Book* when all the ancient ruins started collapsing around him. My arms and legs had gone stiff, but my insides were all flapping and diving like a kite in the wind.

Dead.

Dead!

Dead?

I knew what being dead was and I wanted to ask questions like when and how and why, but I was too scared, especially as Mum had a right face on her and Martin was slamming the kitchen cupboards, saying stuff about 'funny fuckers' and 'child snatchers'. There was a horrible smell of burnt toast. 'Whys there never no fuckin' food in this fuckin' house?'

'Why d'you have to go and open your big mouth?'

'What?'

'It's a fuckin' kid, that's what!'

And then Martin started on about 'a fuckin' dosshouse'. I didn't understand what that was, but I knew by the way they were carrying on that this business about Little Daryl was serious and he hadn't just gone on holiday or moved houses.

That's when I started thinking that if Daryl was dead, maybe the same thing would happen to me. After all, we went to the same school and played together on the same street and were both the same age. We were seven.

I'd heard people say that seven's supposed to be a lucky number. But it wasn't lucky for Daryl, was it?! And I didn't feel all that lucky, although I suppose things weren't too bad. Mum had her new boyfriend, Martin, and the house was always filled with their friends, Earl and Fat Davey, as well as Colette from next door. The door was always knocking and the phone was always ringing. Our living room was like one of those poncey restaurants I'd seen on *Newsround*, where a conveyor belt winds past you and then back out through the kitchen. Except there weren't any animals or fashionable foreign food in our house. Just sweaty visitors decked out in leather jackets and earrings and dodgy hairstyles. And they'd always arrive clutching a bottle of Buckfast, wrapped in green crepe paper, fresh from the off-licence, or 'the offie' as they used to call it. I watched our houseguests closely when they arrived because one of them would sometimes bring a Curly Wurly or a polystyrene aeroplane for me.

For those who've managed to avoid it, Buckfast is a kind of strong red wine, brewed by monks in Devon. In Scotland, it's known as a bottle of 'What the hell are you looking at?' and people say things like 'Buckfast gets you fucked fast'. I was a 'Buckie baby', born to the smell and taste of it: I first sampled the ruby nectar when my dummy was dipped in a glass and, when I got older, I'd sip the syrupy dregs I could find in the mornings. Its fruity flavour was as familiar to me as a cup of tea, and the phrase 'nip down the offie for a bottle of Buckie' was one I heard often.

My dad didn't live with us, although he sometimes came over on the weekends. But only when he wasn't busy. He wasn't even there when I was born, though he turned up at the hospital afterwards. He must've felt bad about it because he said to my mum, 'You can choose the name if you like.' She chose Dustin, but my dad said it sounded like dustbin. So, then he went, 'Call him Spike if you want, or Tarquin. Or Carl... You can call him Carl.'

Mum was alright with that, so she called me Carl. And for some reason, people started calling me Carlos, which was then shortened to Lossie. I could have been called much worse things, so I didn't mind the nickname, but I was a bit worried that it sounded like lassie, which is a Scottish word for a girl, or Lofty, who was a weedy bloke off of *EastEnders*. We never, ever missed an episode of *EastEnders*. We'd all get in front of the telly to watch Michelle and Lofty and Wicksy and Dirty Den as if they were our own family.

When the TV wasn't on, my mum'd be playing her records. She had loads of records. There was one called 'Love of the Common People' and I liked it because the singer, Paul Young, came from Luton, like me. And if you turned the record over, it had a different song called 'Wherever I Lay My Hat, That's My Home'. The music in our house was varied—reggae, rock, soul, punk, pop—and it all percolated its way into me. I loved smelling the vinyl and looking at the cardboard sleeves. *Sgt Pepper's* was a carnival of piercing colours and *Thriller* came with a set of 3D glasses. I have sweet early memories of being with my mum during the daytime before I'd started at school. There'd be no one else around and it was like we'd formed our own secret little band. The TV would be off, Mum would have her music on, and she'd be bopping her feet from side to side and wiggling her hips while cleaning. I'd be on the floor, drumming on an empty biscuit tin, pretending to be Ringo Starr. Before I could even write my own name, I knew the names of all The Beatles from studying the album sleeve of *Help!*

So, there was always music in our home and there were always people, and so, as a little squirt with sticky-out ears and a round face, I was petted and made a fuss of and always the centre of attention.

But all that stuff was before. Before I heard the thing about Little Daryl. Before I started wondering what could make a kid dead.

Chapter 2
Wot, No Meat?

My dad left was six months old. Mum said it was because he was too friendly with the nurses at the hospital where he worked. I'm close to my mum and she's sort of like a superhero to me because she's always worked hard and done the best she could.

Excerpt from an autobiography I wrote for a school project when I was thirteen. Modestly titled: The Secret of My Success.

November 2019

I'm being pursued, hunted down by a disgusting demon. A parasitic predator with sharp fangs and claws that hides in the shadows, snarling. It crouches over my bed at 3 a.m. and snaps me awake. It inhabits my body, crushing me from within. It burrows deep into the core of my very being, bleeding my energy. It gets inside my head and taunts me. It whispers negative remarks, vicious threats, and vile insults. It tells me to hate myself.

I know I should ignore it. My good fortune surrounds me. I've got a nice house and a nice car. I have a loving wife, two beautiful children who tell me they love me, and a wide circle of people who seem to like me. They say I'm lucky, but guess what? I'm having none of it. I'm not fortunate. I'm a fraud, an impostor who should be somewhere else. I'm experiencing all these strange things that I don't understand.

It's a Saturday afternoon and I've climbed up into the loft to fetch a dusty cardboard box with Kodak written on the sides. It contains old letters, magazines, and loose photographs, and I'm sifting through it in the desperate hope that I'll discover something relating to my old childhood friend Little Daryl. Something, anything, that will tell me what happened to him and why. I find an old photo of me and my mum. She's wearing a black T-shirt and holding me in the doorway of our house and we're both squinting into the sun. She's got a feathered perm and a fag on the go and I'm wearing a green cardigan with trains on it. I must have been about two or three. I put the faded picture down and continue to dig through the piles of paperwork. It's not the first time I've done this and, once again, I discover diddly squat. But I'm more determined than ever this time, so I decide to try the internet. On Google, I type the words 'Daryl', 'child', 'dead', 'Luton', '1980s'. But the search results return nothing. I try changing the word combinations and adding capitals, quotation marks, and hyphens. I use different search engines and browse the results pages further than ever before. But nothing, nada, zilch, zip. Fuck all.

I don't know why I'm looking. I know there's zero information on the web about what happened to Little Daryl. Nonetheless, I sense that familiar disappointment and frustration. Surely, somebody must've known something about it.

I pick up my phone and ring my mum. I dive straight in. 'You remember there was that lad from down our street who got killed?'

'Yeah,' she replies briskly.

'Little Daryl, we called him. D'you remember?'

There's a pause and my mum makes a sound like she's taking a sip of tea. 'Oh, I do. Yeah, you played with him, didn't you? Lived around the corner, but he used to go all over the place. Everyone knew him.' Mum's memory is woolly but I still sense her wanting to change the subject.

'Did he really get killed?'

'I really can't remember much, love. There was a lot of stuff went on on that estate. Burglaries, shootings, stabbings, you name it. That's just how it was. Stuff used to happen all the time.'

'What about the family? Did you—?'

'I knew the mother... What was her name? Didn't know her properly, like. Just to say hello to. Anyway, they must have all moved away 'cos I never heard nothing after.'

I decide not to press it any further and I listen to my mum telling me about her car battery.

***

My mum was born to Ron and Vera in 1959, the eldest of three sisters who wore identical Crimplene pinafore dresses. A lady called Babs who lived down the street had hand-stitched the floral print fabrics. Both her sisters had bouncy blonde hair which was cropped short, but my mum's hair was dark and straight. Even as a child, Zoe had insisted on being different and begged her parents to allow her to grow her hair longer. Eventually, they gave permission, but the hair could be no longer than shoulder length and it always had to be tied back in a neat ponytail.

Both of Mum's parents came from working-class families from the East End of London who had escaped the Blitz during the Second World War. They worked nine-to-five jobs and benefitted from the economic growth of the 1950s and '60s. Eventually, they purchased a house on the high street that was on the edge of our estate and set to work on constructing a traditional conservative family. Ron and Vera were, in my eyes, the perfect image of suburban normalcy and respectability. It also meant that while my grandparents loved me—I knew this because of the Christmas and birthday presents they always sent—I sensed they had certain opinions of my mum's young pregnancy, her subsequent single motherhood, and our council house lifestyle. They were young grandparents: only in their forties or fifties and busy with their respective lives. Vera was a prim secretary who drove a red Mini. She smoked a single Silk Cut cigarette once a year, after her Christmas dinner. Ron smoked John Player Specials and drove a vinyl-topped Ford Capri. He wore Old Spice aftershave, a leather jacket, and driving gloves. Much of his professional life was shrouded in secrecy. All the rest of us knew was that he was employed as a draftsman for a firm which specialized in technical drawings and that was it. It was many years later that we learned Ron had spent his career in a secure compound, working on various top-secret nuclear warhead projects.

Ron and Vera divorced when I was three, but they both kept spotless houses with cream carpets and placemats and little bowls of potpourri sat on glass tables. Not the sorts of places you would want sticky-faced children hanging around. Plus, Ron was usually too busy travelling abroad or running around with different girlfriends to host me. He didn't exactly fit the traditional grandad image from the Werther's Original ads. He was much more the Milk Tray man.

Ron occasionally came over to drop a birthday card. Sometimes, he'd do the 'poke 'n' run', which is to say, I'd hear the flap of card coming through the letterbox and, by the time I'd gone over to the window to see who it was, I'd just catch the back of my granddad's Capri hurtling down the street. On the rare occasion that either of the grandparents ventured inside our house, my mum and whoever was visiting would frantically tear around the place, snatching up the drug paraphernalia. The record sleeves that were covered in golden tobacco debris and stray skins would be slid under the sofa and the dope went in a wooden box on top of the gas fire. Neither grandparent ever stayed for very long.

My mum had grown up in an ordered household, in an era when children were taught to be mindful of their manners and to be seen and not heard. So, when she flew the nest aged sixteen, she decided to make her own rules. She didn't want to be a typist like her mother, so she went to art college and later became a vegetarian: a fairly rare thing in the 1980s. One time, Mum prepared us an omelette salad for tea. I stared down at the plate for a few seconds and then I turned towards my mum, scrunched up my face, and repeated the words 'Wot, no meat? Wot no meat?' It was a line from a popular TV ad at the time, and it became a standing joke in our house, one which we repeated whenever Mum gave us vegetables.

Mum wasn't much of a cook, usually cobbling together functional items from the freezer such as fish fingers, peas, and chips slathered in red sauce. But she *was* creative with her concoctions. At Easter, she made dippy eggs and soldiers and she'd channel her artistic talent by drawing funny faces on the shells of the eggs. Also, she had a rabbit-shaped jelly mould and would sometimes make corned beef faces. The pulpy pink canned meat was sliced and carefully positioned in the centre of the plate and, depending on what was available, she used chips or mashed potato for the hair, beans for the mouth and nose, and maybe two slices of cucumber for the eyes. Corned beef faces may have been a cunning ploy to get me to consume the leftover scraps from the pantry but, also, they were an example of the special effort and attention to detail that only a cash-strapped parent can concoct.

My mum was seventeen when she met my dad. He made her laugh. He was an older man who worked as a porter at the local hospital; a groovy cat who drank barley wine and lime, wore ripped trousers, and had long dark hair which fell in ringlets almost to his waist. Zoe was different: clean and bright and girlishly pretty, with a fringe which sat neatly over her big eyes. She had a luminance about her: the curious fizz of somebody who is not yet sure what they will become. Shortly after meeting my dad, she dropped out of art college and ended up working on the checkout at Tescos. The pair lived together in various shared lodgings before marrying in January 1979. As a newly married couple, they were given their first council house, and I was born a year later. The breakup must have come shortly afterwards as I have no memory of them together and don't know if they had happy times. If they did, I never saw them and, to my knowledge, not a single photograph exists of them together.

Dexys Midnight Runners were at number one on the day I was born. My mum had been home alone and didn't have a phone, so she traipsed down to the hospital by herself without telling anyone she was about to give birth. Besides, it was the day of her cousin Andy's funeral, so most of her family were out. Andy had died in a car accident exactly two weeks previously, aged eighteen. It was never really ascertained what had caused their vehicle to skid off the road and collide with a tree but the impact had been enough to bring Andy's young life to a swift and tragic halt.

It was the early hours of that Saturday morning when I came into the world screaming. It hadn't been a straightforward delivery: I was a breech birth and I was yellow from jaundice and purple from a lack of oxygen. The doctors whipped me away from my mum and put me in an incubator.

Even though my dad worked at the same hospital, he was nowhere to be seen. Mum didn't know it yet, but she was destined to join the stone-washed squadron of single mothers who marched on the estate with their pushchairs and permed hair. Dressed in light blue denim and going to and from the local shops, or lining up outside the clinic to seek reassurance from the nurse about the growing list of ailments their babies had developed. Colic, nappy rash, water on the testicles, hernia of the belly button: I had them all.

Within a couple of months, my mum found herself completely alone, with a new baby and little help from friends or family. It was the first time she had been responsible for a set of male genitalia and she didn't know what to do with them. The doctors were unsupportive and there were no mobile phones or internet, so she borrowed books from the library to ease the anxieties around her sickly child's post-natal gripes.

By the time I was about four, the pressures of being a new parent wore off and my mum would stop off at the local pub to chat with the other single mums. The Man on Wheels, it was called. I used to sit outside on the pale brick wall and stare at the sign creaking and swinging on a tall post above: it had a picture of a man and a penny-farthing on it. The Man on Wheels was a lively boozer and the hangout of various mobs and tribes: skinheads, goths, bikers, and punks all coexisted peacefully. But gangs of undesirables, with names like The MIGs (Men in Gear) and the BOLTs (Boys of Luton Town) attended the pub, also, and brought trouble. They were notorious yobbos. I remember seeing their tags scrawled on the walls and pillars around the estate. Apparently, at the end of every Friday night, they used to put on a record called 'I Love the Sound of Breaking Glass' and then proceed to smash the place up. The violence, drugs, and underage drinking eventually got too much for the succession of landlords and the establishment closed its doors permanently in 1988. I heard that the final straw was when a disgruntled patron drove a JCB into the building. Someone else said it was an arson attack. Either way, the pub never reopened and the site was later cleared to make way for more social housing.

Everyone in our community knew my mum. Of course, I didn't see it, but it must have been because she was beautiful. Not the heels and make-up type of beautiful—she didn't have time for that—although she did draw darting glances and wolf whistles from the winos who sat on the wall over the shops. (Supposedly, they voted her best-looking girl on the estate for three years on the trot.) She was a different kind of beautiful. Beautiful in the way that she took the time to stop to talk to people. All sorts of people. Even the locals who everyone else tried to avoid, like Mad Jack, Rasta Joe, and Carol, the middle-aged deaf girl who stood outside the Co-op every day. My mum would stand there for ages, in all weathers, listening to their nonsense. No one ever nicked the milk from her doorstep, either, because 'she was alright, she was'.

It was on the August bank holiday of 1982 that my mum took me to a summer fete at a local park. Rock bands were playing on the back of a truck and Zoe was enjoying the music when, somehow, I must have escaped from her sight and we became separated. A stranger spotted me wandering amongst the throng of people and handed me to a policeman who gave me a lollipop to keep me happy while he sought to reunite me with my young mum.

I don't know how long I was lost but I guess I was lucky the kind stranger found me or I might have ended up somewhere else. And like my mum said, 'a lot of stuff went on on that estate'. Of course, I don't remember wandering solo around the fete or being picked up by the policeman, but I know it happened because, in amongst the box of old memories, I found a newspaper cutting with the caption 'PC's long arm protects a lost youngster', accompanied by a picture of me and the burly copper. The journalist from the local rag must've spotted us and thought we'd make a good photo-op. I was wearing a stylish double-breasted leather coat which my mum had bought from the jumble sale that same day.

People often stopped my mum to tell her how adorable I looked, with my rosy cheeks, baby blond curls, and bright blue eyes, and I enjoyed being the subject of their conversations. I was a confident little kid, clueless of the fact that I would spend many more miserable hours rummaging around second-hand clothes shops with my mum, like the time when I was due to start infant school. Leagrave Infants, it was called, and it stood on the same street as Leagrave Junior School. Infants wasn't a big school like Juniors, but I still had to wear a uniform: a shirt and tie. Mum got vouchers to help towards the cost of the school uniforms, and I was jazzed when we went downtown on the bus to get a new set of crisp white shirts and woolly grey trousers from C&A. Going downtown was nearly always a fun experience, but this school uniform outing was where the fun ended.

Mum was pregnant with her third child, and she was rubbing her big belly as she waded through the racks of clothes which dangled from their wire hangers. She pressed a few items up against my skinny frame before deciding on the ones she wanted for me. I didn't like her doing that but then I saw my reflection in the mirror and imagined how smart I'd look on my first day at school. Mum folded the school uniforms over her arm, plucked a pack of blue polyester Y-fronted underpants and some flannel socks from the shelf, and led me towards the checkout. I was holding on to the plastic handle of the buggy, my little sister, Sophie, swaddled snugly inside, as my mum was getting ready to hand the coupons over when she put her hand up to her face.

'You alright?' the cashier went.

'Yeah, just a bit hot,' my mum replied before mumbling something about not feeling very well.

All of a sudden, my mum dropped to the floor. It looked like that horrible bit in *The Wizard of Oz* when the green-faced witch shrivels up into a pile of clothes, except Zoe wasn't shrieking that she was melting. She was silent, her eyes were shut, and she was lying still on the grey carpet. The coupons and the uniform were lying in a heap beside her and the shop assistants were flapping about, trying to help. I'd seen something like this happen on the telly and it didn't end well.

'Is she dead? Is she dead? Is she dead?' I said, looking from one adult to the next. I got no answer, so I gripped the buggy tighter and sucked up the salty snot and tears. 'Is she dead?'

Still no answer. So, I started whimpering 'Leave my mum alone!' at the waists of the strangers who were all fussing around my lifeless mother.

I felt stiff like I couldn't walk, and loads of questions were clanging through my head at the same time: *Why's everyone ignoring me? Have they killed my mum? What about my school uniform? Will an ambulance be called? What will happen to me?* I didn't give a single thought to the unborn baby inside my mum's belly or my sister who was sitting quietly the whole time.

Eventually, my mum opened her eyes and the strangers helped her up. They were picking up her things and being all nice. Then they made us go outside. I didn't know what to say, so I just stood there in the breezy shop doorway, holding onto my mum like a limpet. Her face was pale as she sat on a folding chair, sipping water from a paper cup. Zoe looked at me and brushed my hair aside with her clammy hand. 'I'm alright,' she said, 'I only fainted.' I didn't really know what 'only fainted' meant, and I didn't ask because I was just glad she was still alive.

Then my mum sprung up from the chair and gathered up her shopping bags. She'd spotted the number five bus as it came hurtling around the corner towards our stop.

Seeing my mum collapse like that got me thinking about how a person could just fall down and not be alive anymore. And then, they'd be gone and you'd be all by yourself, not knowing what to do. That idea frightened and worried me. I wasn't used to being frightened yet. I had no idea that seeing my mum fainting was only a tiny taste of the terrors that were to come. Of what was to befall poor Little Daryl.

Chapter 3

We Need to Talk About Emrys

My old man's a dustman, he wears a dustman's hat. He farted through the keyhole and paralyzed the cat.

Playground rhyme

Emrys is an old family name of Welsh origin. It means immortal. It was my Welsh grandfather's hated first name and then my father's, too. It's my hated middle name and my son also bears the brand. I didn't want to do it but I felt compelled to give him the name. Whenever you tell people your name is Emrys, they lean in closer and say, 'What? Hendrix?' or '*Everest?* Like Mount Everest?' Despite our inexplicable decision to keep the name, the four generations have often hidden it or even flat out denied it. For this reason, my grandad was known as

Eddie to his comrades during the war, while my dad settled on telling schoolmates that his name was Elvis, like Elvis Presley.

Emrys Meek Jr, my father, was a spidery man who took long strides when he walked, thrusting out his crazy denim-clad legs as if he were bounding over a dog turd. Emrys underwent many incarnations throughout his life, from long-haired hippy to his final adornment of a cowboy hat and an oxygen mask. You never really think of your parents as handsome or good-looking but I suppose he was when he was younger, with a crop of thick dark hair and slightly downwardly angled light blue eyes which lent a sort of intelligent kindness to his long lean face.

He grew up in Luton and left school at fifteen. In the 1960s, you had the option to continue in education or you were given a list of jobs from which you had to choose a trade. My dad hated school and feared manual labour but he *was* interested in fashion, so he ran his spindly index finger down the page and chose a barbering apprenticeship. Young Emrys spent long days on his feet, making perpetual cups of tea and sweeping mounds of hair into a little cupboard. On the weekends, my dad attended youth dances at Luton Boys' Club and The Odeon. He reckoned he and his sister Eileen saw The Beatles there in 1963. The Beatles did play in Luton, but Eileen says they never saw them. Rock music was evolving and making its mark on popular culture, and Emrys Junior continually pestered his parents to buy him a guitar. Eileen had received a typewriter the previous year, so their mum and dad relented eventually. It arrived in time for his fifteenth birthday and, although teenage Emrys never learned to play the guitar properly, he loved that stringed instrument. My dad would often stay up late in his room, listening to music and strumming his guitar. As a result, he was notoriously bad at getting up, so his mum had to come up to his room every morning to wake him. She resorted to many different tactics to try to prise him from his warm pit, from throwing water in his face to putting a lit cigarette in his mouth. One day, Emrys's mother went to his bedroom four times until she finally snapped. She marched into the room and picked up the first thing she saw: the guitar leaning upright in the corner. His mother grabbed the thing by the neck and swung it gracefully through the air like a woodcutter bearing an axe down on a log. She smashed the guitar squarely over my old man's head and his hard dome went clean through the thin wooden casing. He sat bolt up in his bed, cuckoos flying over his head and the broken strings twanging around his neck.

By 1968, The Beatles' music was becoming more experimental—it was the year they released 'While My Guitar Gently Weeps'. It was also the year that my dad started on the wacky-backy. He was sixteen. I think that this may have marked the point when Emrys decided that he wasn't going to play by the rest of the world's rules. He blamed it on peer pressure but the teenage decision to take an experimental dip into the evolving counterculture was a defining moment in my dad's life. He said that he'd wanted to be one of the cool kids, and that was why he spent much of his spare time spaced out, listening to psychedelic rock music.

Different varieties of cannabis affect different people in different ways. For many, the primary effects are that it induces pleasure, heightens senses, and stimulates creativity. For some people, it may calm them, ease pain, and aid relaxation. For others, it can stupefy or make you paranoid and depressed. For my dad, it may have done any of these things but, primarily, it rendered him lazy, a slowpoke, a procrastinator. When puffing on the Devil's lettuce, he would stagnate and drift off into a fantasy world where his responsibilities and his motivation would take a back seat. Emrys would recline on the couch and dream up fantastical schemes that he was, then, incapable of putting into motion. It was as though his body became bound by a relaxing spell: with one hand, he was given great ideas and aspirations; but with the other, the power of execution was sucked away from him. Like being gently eased into a comforting straitjacket where your sense of duty and your ability to perform physical tasks somehow evaporate with the smoke.

Emrys's love affair with Mary Jane began with reefers and evolved to edibles, bongs, pipes, vapes, hotboxing, growing, and selling. Cannabis became his obsession and by the time Emrys reached his twenties, he had decided to turn his back on the mainstream and become a full-on joint-smoking hippy. He grew his hair long and quit his job at the barber's. His parents wouldn't let him live at home unless he worked, so my dad found a job working as a porter at the Luton and Dunstable

Hospital ...right across the road. My dad said he enjoyed the job. He wore an unbuttoned lab coat and carried a pager, and around his neck hung a 'borrowed' stethoscope that he used as a prop for flirting with the nurses. 'Trust me, I'm a doctor,' he would say while swinging around the dangly end of the device.

My dad was handsome and charismatic and so well-liked among all the other hospital workers, he rose to the position of head porter and union rep. The union recognized his gift of the gab and Emrys was offered an opportunity to work for them at a senior level but he turned it down. My dad's popularity meant he had many friends and he spent much of his time 'working late' or partying in the nurses' quarters. One friend, in particular, a pretty, brown-skinned student nurse, would call at our house. If Emrys wasn't there, she'd lurk around the corner behind a lamppost, intermittently peeking around, waiting for him to arrive home. My father had long been failing to control his impulses and it wasn't long before he decided to leave.

But like I said, I still saw my dad. Sometimes. And, as a nosey five-year-old, I earwigged in on his conversations and got to know the difference between indica, sativa, Moroccan hashish, high-grade green, Sensi skunk, Indian black, Lebanese blonde, Thai sticks, Jamaican ganja and homegrown grass. It was around me all the time and I became very familiar with the sweet, sickly smell of weed burning in a joint, accompanied by the narrowed eyes and the creepy smiles on the adults smoking it. The distinctive eerie clouds hovered gently above their heads like ghosts as they played a game called 'Pass the Doobie'.

I was sitting on the couch next to my dad one evening as he was putting the finishing touches on one of his special cigarettes. He was hunched over like an insect as he neatly assembled his skins, heated his bit of dope, and sprinkled it onto the tobacco. Now, he seemed to be concentrating hard, poking around with his nimble fingers at what looked like pencil shavings in a little paper boat. Then he licked all the way along the edge of the paper and carefully wrapped it up into a delicate cone. After that, he slotted a roach into the thin end, smoothed out all the wrinkles, and twisted the fat end into a little hairstyle. Emrys inspected his work, holding it up and massaging its long sleek body. He seemed pleased that there was no bagginess to it. He placed the pointy end into his mouth and popped his lighter. The long flame licked the twisty hairstyle, which immediately flared up, illuminating Emrys' face like a glowworm. It made a hiss and sputtered as he took his first toke. My dad held the smoke in for a second or two, but he must have seen me watching because he pulled the cone away from his mouth. I noticed he was still holding his breath as he pinched the joint between his thumb and forefinger like a penny whistle.

'You don't never talk about this to no one, boy. Not a dickie bird, alright?! 'Specially not to them nosey, prying bloody teachers.' Emrys was slowly exhaling as he spoke, and his narrowed eyes were looking straight at me. The thick smoke was pouring off the end of his joint and curling into my face. 'This stuff's against the law and if any of them meddling teachers find out about it, me and your mum'll both go to prison.'

I nodded. I already knew that anyway. He'd sworn me to lifelong secrecy and I'd carried that heavy burden with me for as long as I could remember. I became jittery when I heard words like pot, grass, blow, dope, and joint, even in everyday contexts. It was around this time I saw an advert on TV telling people to 'just say no' to drugs. But I figured it only applied to America where all the kids had white trainers and skateboards and an unlimited supply of Pepsi Cola in their fridges. It couldn't have been here because we hardly ever had Pepsi and *here* everyone was just saying 'yes' to the drugs.

Pretty much all the adults I knew smoked marijuana. My dad was on another level, though. Emrys worshipped the sacred plant like an Amazonian shaman. He rigged up elaborate hydroponic systems to grow it wherever he could and he cross-pollinated plants to breed hybrid profiles with cool-sounding names like Northern Lights and Super Haze. My dad even travelled to Holland a couple of times a year to sneak back new strains of seeds in his ass. His friends saw him as an authority, a mogul of marijuana, a connoisseur of cannabis, a knower of narcotics, a spliffical wise wizard. Me, on the other hand? Well, I once saw him on his hands and knees in the bathroom, carefully sifting through his own shit to find his smuggled seeds. In my eyes, he was a pothead, a stoner, and a criminal.

It worried me what my dad did. But I suppose I was lucky, in a way, because some of the kids I knew didn't even have dads. They'd either never met them or they lived far apart. Still, I didn't feel like I fitted in with the kids who *did* have dads. They sometimes played a game called 'My Dad's Better Than Your Dad' where they would brag about how strong their old man was or what kind of car he drove or what job he did. Whenever people asked me what my dad's job was (which was more often than I liked), I used to invent plant-related professions for him, like herbalist or horticultural engineer. Something long and boring like that would usually make the question go away. Sometimes, I'd say my dad worked at the nearby Vauxhall factory. Heck, I'd have willingly donned a flat cap and danced a merry jig while singing a cockney rendition of 'My Old Man's a Dustman'. At least it would have meant he had a job.

On my fifth birthday, my dad took me to a caff in the Luton Arndale Centre. We were sitting at a sticky table in one of the stained-glass smoking booths and the waitress brought me out a knickerbocker glory. It came in a tall glass with a long spoon and it had a cherry and a sparkler stuck in the top. I ate 'til my tummy ached and I still couldn't finish it all.

Another of the fond recollections I have with him was when he took me to the cinema to see *101 Dalmatians*. It was another of those rare and wonderful times when it was just me and him. I sat cradled in the too-big, scratchy, fold-down chair, tucking into a packet of sweet powdery milk bottles, looking up intermittently at the screen to see an evil skeleton-faced woman who was trying to kill puppies.

On other occasions, we went to a sour-smelling pub where I'd stand in a corner wrestling with a snooker cue. Or if they didn't allow children in, I'd sit on a bench outside sipping a Coke.

But regardless of where Emrys took me, he always brought me back late. I'd get tired and irritable before the end and if it was past midnight, which it usually was, my mum would be pissed off because she worked hard to create a routine for me.

One of the places my dad most liked to bring me was to his job at the hospital so he could proudly show me off to all his mates. I've often heard people say that they find going to hospitals unpleasant, worrying or sickening, but I don't. I enjoyed going there, especially to the canteen where I watched the TV and ate chips. And even today, the bustle and beeps of the nurse's station, the strong odours of industrial disinfectant employed to mask the odours of illness and death, trolleys gliding through the endless silent corridors, walls adorned with sun-bleached paintings of lilies... All this is a calming experience for me.

I'd go on to spend more time at the hospital with my dad, regularly visiting his second son in the children's ward. My half-brother Riki was born with acute asthma and he had many episodes during his childhood. I even ended up working as a porter myself at the same hospital some fifteen years later while I was studying at university. My colleagues were a cross-section of nutters, numbskulls, and nincompoops and the pay sucked, but it was probably the best job I've ever had.

Sadly, my dad eventually quit his job at the hospital. It was deep in the Thatcher era and Emrys had decided that he no longer wanted to work for the Man and that he was going to go it alone. By coincidence, this decision happened to come shortly after my mum started asking him for child support. The truth is that Emrys believed that paying child maintenance would send him into financial ruin, so he hung up his white coat and never worked again. It's a truth which has been a hard pill for me to swallow as my father was a dazzlingly intellectual and funny man. He came from a generation that wanted to change the world but his idle tendencies and his addictions meant that his life wafted into a purple haze.

I loved my dad. He's part of me and I'm part of him. He had his faults but he was kind and he loved me, too. I know this because, despite his failings, he was there for me. Emrys always showed up late and stoned...but he showed up. Not like all the other dads who lived far away. Or the stepdads who would come and go, and you wouldn't know if they were gonna give you a Kinder Surprise or a clip around the ear. I'd heard talk about my mum's boyfriend Martin being my stepdad but I never wanted one. Besides, I already had a dad and the idea of having two dads confused me.

Little Daryl had told me that his real dad was dead, and now he'd only got a stepdad, so one day, while we were fixing my bike, I decided to ask him about it all.

'What's it like havin' a stepdad?' I asked while spinning the wheel of my upturned BMX.

'I dunno,' he said, poking a stick at the metal rods so it rumbled. 'Alright, I s'pose.'

'But why's it called a stepdad?

'Huh?'

'Is it 'cos they just *step* inside your house and pretend to be your dad, so they can tell you off whenever they want?'

'Yeah, you can say that again.' Daryl giggled. But I didn't say it again, I just kept quiet. 'You wouldn't wanna get on the wrong side of yer stepdad, though. You have to behave yourself like, then he'll prob'ly look out for ya. And he'll take you out and that. Might even get you stuff...even if he does do bad things sometimes.' The tip of Daryl's tongue peeked out the corner of his mouth as he raised his arm and inspected the graze on his elbow that was starting to form a scab.

I didn't know what else to say, so I pumped the pedal on my bicycle until the wheels were spinning really, really fast. Daryl's words sounded again in my head: '*You have to behave yourself like, then he'll prob'ly look out for ya.*'

What, like a mate? I thought. But what sort of a mate would do bad things to you? That made me think that I wanted a stepdad even less.

And it made me a bit fearful for my friend who was now staring at the bike wheel, waiting for the perfect moment to jam his bit of wood into the swirling silver spokes.

Chapter 4

Earl and Fat Daisy

Fatty and Skinny were in the bath,
Fatty blew off and made Skinny laugh.

Playground rhyme

Not far from our house, there was a big sign that said 'Welcome to Luton'. Most people think that there's nothing at all that welcoming about Luton, which frequently appears in the polls as one of the worst towns in Britain. But growing up, I wasn't aware of any of that. I was perfectly contented in my little hometown which I'd learned had been there since 'the olden times'. Luton used to be famous for making straw hats until boater hats fell out of fashion and machines took over. In 1905, the Vauxhall car factory was opened in Luton. It became the biggest car maker in the country, with thousands of employees. So, during the '50s and '60s, even more businesses opened and people came from Asia and the Caribbean to work there. The place grew and changed from a few folks making straw hats to a sprawling town of about two hundred thousand people, an equal mix of black, white, and Asian.

At the north end of Luton, there are three almost identical housing estates, easily identified by the half dozen baby-crap-brown-coloured tower blocks which jut out of the landscape. They can be seen for miles around (or, at least, from the northbound carriageway of the M1 motorway). Ours was just like any other normal estate. Hockwell Ring, it was called. It was known locally as The Ring because of how the main street arced its way around the parade of shops and the flats like the ring pull off a Coke can. The Ring was, and still is, located between two other areas called Marsh Farm and Lewsey Farm, which were both named after the arable land on which they were constructed. All three council estates were built just after the war to provide prefabricated homes for all the people arriving from London and abroad.

Our first family home was on Pirton Road. It was a plain terraced house with square windows, a blue front door, and gingerbread-coloured bricks. Add a yellow sun and a couple of ms in the sky to look like birds and it looked exactly how it did in my two-dimensional drawings. Our house was at the rough end of the street that backed onto railway tracks and the River Lea. It was the second-from-last house, squished in between the two identical houses on either side, with a narrow alley which tunnelled through the middle to the back gardens.

The old lady who shared our alley was called Colette. She was a bag of bones, draped in skin which looked like it had been pickled. Colette was an older woman who'd had a hard life in Ireland. But she was friendly enough, with her big glasses and her perfectly polished fingernails on the ends of her lizard-y hands. She often came around ours to borrow important things like cigarettes or tea bags and, sometimes, I got sent over to her house, which smelt like smoky bacon crisps but was always spotless.

When she wasn't dipping into our house, Colette could be found down at The Cement Shed. After the closure of the Man on Wheels pub, The Cement Shed was the only place on the estate where you could get a drink. It was a long building with barred windows and it was always dark inside. And lined along the cracked leatherette benches, there would be a handful of hardened drinkers with glum faces and purple noses, silently sipping their beverages.

Our front door was always open, so I spent much of my time playing outside, watched over by the neighbours who lingered on doorsteps sipping cups of tea. I roamed freely up and down the road, safe in the knowledge that I knew everyone on our street and they all knew me. The closeness of the houses and the joined-up strip of front yards which we treated as common land fostered a close sense of community.

The house was lived in by me and my mum...and whoever else happened to be there at the time. There was always a steady train of visitors, and I was often left in the care of the various people passing through. My earliest memories are of having my hair ruffled by the stooping shadows of cheerful visitors. And boogie-down beats. And in the morning, the bleary eyes and the bitter Buckfast breath of a houseguest who'd spent the night on our sofa.

One such houseguest was Earl. He was more of a lodger than a houseguest; sometimes he was there and sometimes he wasn't. I remember being taken for a ride in the back of Earl's big van. We were going to the hospital to collect my mum who had just given birth to my sister, Sophie. I was excited about the arrival of the new baby, who brought more life and joy into our house. Sophie was a quiet, contented child who played nicely with her ponies and fell into a deep sleep whenever our mum put the Hoover around. In the months after, she grew into a chubby toddler and we slept in the same room. We played together and splashed around in the shared bathtub. She looked to me for direction, but I prodded her fat little legs and yanked the dummy from her mouth.

I can remember coming downstairs on a Sunday morning; I must have been around four. Sophie was chasing the cat around the hallway in her baby walker as I padded barefoot onto the black-and-white lino in the kitchen. There was no door—just some rainbow-coloured plastic strips hanging from the frame above. I liked how they brightened up the house and danced gently in the wind when the windows were open. Sometimes, my mum would give me a vitamin from the big glass jar with cotton wool in it. But this time, Earl was there instead, in his pants and leaning against the fridge. He was smiling while holding a mug of tea and a fag in the same hand. Earl had a bony Herman Munster-shaped head and a huge pink Adam's apple protruding from his thicker-than-average neck. His name was Earl but I called him Ell. I'd heard that his father, Rex, had been a violent man who frightened the family. Earl had an older brother called Duke and a younger brother named Gary. I guess they must've run out of tough-guy names by the time Gary was born.

'Alright, Lossie, know any swear words?' Earl bowed his bony head to light another cigarette off the cooker.

'Fuck,' I piped, followed by, 'shit.'

'Yeah!' Earl leaned back on the counter and blew a ball of smoke. His smile had turned into a strange grin. They were the only two words I could think of. It was Earl's turn. He rattled off a few I hadn't heard of: bitch, bollocks, cunt, prick...

'Fuckin' 'ell,' I squealed. I was pleased with myself. 'Get it? FUCKIN'...'ELL...'

Earl's elocution lessons might not have been taught in the traditional way but they certainly had an impact on me. I've always liked using colourful language and my mum said that when I was small, I cursed like a sailor, effing and jeffing from my pram. She even had to buy me a toy fox so she could reassure people that I was saying 'fox' instead of 'fuck'.

And then there was the time my mum gave me a warning.

'If you keep on saying them naughty words, I'm gonna wash yer mouth out with a cake of soap.'

'A cake of soap? Ha!' That sounded more like a treat than a punishment. I wanted to see if she'd follow through, so I swore again.

'Right, that's it.' Zoe wrapped her hand tightly around my wrist, digging her nails in, and led me upstairs to the bathroom where she quickly lathered up a soap stub with a flannel and some water from the tap. She poked the foamy flannel past my pursed lips and rubbed it over my rigid tongue until I started burping and blowing out a sea of bubbles and saliva.

The soap cake wasn't all that bad but it didn't taste like any cake I'd ever had. Tasted more like earwax and old-lady perfume. Anyway, it was that Fucking Ell's fault, I decided. He was the one who taught me to swear.

Fucking Ell was mostly charming, and he'd have this shifty glint in his eyes when he was around my mum. Earl often had red blotches on his thick neck, which his son said were called love bites. Uuuck!

Earl's son was called Craig and he sometimes came over to play. I liked Craig, partly because he had a Subbuteo set but, also, because he was similar to me. Not similar in how we looked—Craig had a freckled face and a skinhead with a rat's tail at the back—but in how we were used to being around lots of adults. Plus, we both knew how to build a fort behind the sofa. A fort that was our own little world, separate from all the music and the drinking. We'd play there together until late, overseen by the backs of the grown-ups' heads that bobbed about when they laughed.

Craig was older than me, so I experienced a pang of jealousy when I'd get sent to bed early and he was allowed to stay up. I'd lie in my bed, wondering whether he'd still be there in the morning, and to my delight, I'd often come downstairs the next day to find him and his dad stretched out on the sofa, which meant our games could continue.

But it wasn't always fun and games. Earl was prone to fits of fury, so Craig had to be careful what he did and said. Any slight incident could cause Earl to ignite like a whistling rocket. Sometimes, Craig had only so much as to fart loudly and his dad would be on him. When this happened, I'd freeze and Craig would run away, skipping and darting in different directions. Occasionally, the boy managed to evade him but if his dad caught him, Craig would be subject to a good hiding.

I was about five years old the first time I became the target of one of Earl's crazy outbursts. It was the summer of 1985 and we had all been driven to Glastonbury in the back of Earl's van. We stopped down a country lane and let some of our passengers out so they could climb the fence, then we drove inside the festival and set up our big orange tent. There were all these freaky punk-rocker types floating around. Craig was there, too, with some older boys but they ran off to the playground before I could catch up. I hung around the campsite, kicking at clumps of grass and staring at all the shirtless beatniks with their beards and funny walks. And there was a song coming from the big speakers. I'd heard it before because my mum had it on record and she'd told me that it was about a little girl who killed some kids at her school and, when they asked the girl why she'd done it, she said it was because she didn't like Mondays. Yikes.

I started thinking about why she would do such a terrible thing, and I imagined that it must be quite easy to kill a kid if a little girl could do it for no real reason. I wanted to ask my mum about it but she'd gone off with Martin. Earl was meant to be looking after me but he was busy skinning up inside his tent. It was a green tent made of faded fabric. Not the shiny material that tents are normally made of, but the thick green canvas stuff that they used to make army clothes. Earl's tent had a few tears in it and, as a big-eared five-year-old, I couldn't resist the temptation of peeping through one of the raggedy holes. Earl saw me from inside the tent and his eyes narrowed like he was reading a faraway sign. He shot out. I didn't even have time to run away, so I just stood there, stiff like one of Craig's Subbuteo men. Earl's eyes bulged and his face was red like an angry spacehopper. Dots of spit hit me in the face as he accused me of ripping his tent. I knew I hadn't ripped his tent but I didn't say anything because I could see that Earl had already made his mind up about it. He held me by the arm and walloped me across my beany buttocks until my thighs throbbed. I wailed and Earl shouted back at me, 'Shullup or I'll give ya summink to cry about.'

My mum used to smack me sometimes. But while I didn't exactly like her smacking me, it was alright because you're allowed to hit your own kids. But not someone else's, right?! Was that what Little Daryl meant about stepdads doing bad things? But that bony-headed fuckin' Ell wasn't even my stepdad. Why was he beating my arse like that? Is that what people do? But then, there were always loads of other people around our house and they never smacked me.

Davey Jones was another one of the regulars at ours. Some people called him Jonesy; others called him Fat Davey, although not to his face. As a young child, I confused the various monikers and called him Fat Daisy. It stuck.

Fat Daisy was a sort of family friend; an uncle who's not your uncle. A bullish black man with a mane of stubby dreads which sprouted from his head like snakes on a gorgon. He had piggy eyes and large brown cheeks which reminded me of Easter eggs. Daisy was one of those fat guys who sweated profusely and carried a flannel in his back pocket to dab the beads of perspiration from his face. His size coupled with his laid-back easy-going demeanour made him appear sluggish but he was deceptively nimble and he could snap into action with terrific speed when required. In fact, Fat Davey Jones was the local bully with a fearsome reputation on our estate and beyond. He particularly enjoyed hogging the back seat of the bus and terrorizing the other passengers.

Fat Daisy was my tormentor and my teacher. He played 'rough and tumble' with me, as well as dominoes. He always won at dominoes but I didn't mind. I just loved lining them up and then slapping the hard-yellow tiles onto my plastic table. And every time he won, Fat Daisy would caw his crazy laugh at me: 'Ke-ke-ke-ke.' It was a high-pitched laugh for a fat man. He liked making other people laugh, too, but he never told stories or jokes. His comedy came in the form of sharp one-liners and outrageous physical acts which were exaggerated by his cartoonish anatomy. He did this thing where, with a quick wiggle of his forefinger, he could flip his eyelids inside out to reveal their veiny pink underside atop the bulging white eyeballs. The spectacle was shocking enough to send my mum scurrying into the hallway and to make me squeal with delight.

My mum told me about the time she placed my dinner on my plastic table and turned around to go back into the kitchen. Daisy saw his opportunity and motioned at me to take the steaming bowl of spaghetti and pour it over my head. Of course, I cooperated, and I was wearing that dinner like a pasta hat when my mum returned to the room.

'Pssshhhhhh! What've you gone and made him do that for, Davey?'

'Ke-ke-ke-ke.'

Although Daisy was an ogre, I respected him. He was entertaining and I loved it when he tossed me up in the air like a football. 'Again, again,' I'd shout.

'Davey, please be gentle with him,' my mum would plead, but that only made Fat Daisy throw me higher.

'Again, again!'

'You make a girl of him and I'll make a man of him,' came Fat Daisy's reply.

I didn't want to be a girl and I knew that Fat Daisy was an expert at being a man. He had immigrated from the island of St Lucia when he was a child, grown up with his mum and his deaf and dumb brother, and he had a daughter called Leona who died of leukaemia when she was eight. Leona had been older than me. I'd met her once when I was small and had been envious when I heard that *Jim'll Fix It* had gone to visit her in the hospital.

One time, I asked Fat Daisy what it was like when he'd first come to England.

'Cold,' he responded flatly.

When I was left alone with Fat Daisy is when I got many of his 'I'll make a man of him' lessons. That blubbery lout would cruelly swipe away my Curly Wurly and eat it in one bite, and if I ever asked him where Mum was, his favourite response was 'Up your bum and 'round the corner', although sometimes he went, 'She's run off with a black man.' And he'd squawk it repeatedly like a macaw, his fat belly wobbling as he laughed. 'Run off with a black man, Run off with a black man. Ke-ke-ke-ke!'

The phrase was particularly cutting as my dad *did* go and live with a black woman when I was a baby. I'd make sure I was a safe distance before I sought my retaliation by wiggling my bum and flapping my arms while singing, 'Hey, Fatty-boom-boom!'

Fat Daisy easily caught me and he'd seize my hand and bend my fingers back toward my forearm. 'Say the magic words,' he'd demand. 'Say 'em!'

But I was stubborn and, while it hurt like hell, I refused to utter the words, secretly promising myself I'd wreak my revenge on Fat Daisy when I got bigger and stronger.

But his favourite game to teach me to be a man was to pin me down under the bulk of his massive gut while I writhed and swam against the dense piles of clammy flesh. I'd withstand for as long as I could in that hot, dark place until I finally had to give in. Only once I was utterly defeated and exhausted, I'd cry out a muffled, 'Mercy, mercy, Uncle Percy!'

Whenever Fat Daisy came around, the first thing he'd do was go over to the stereo and put on his favourite record. He'd turn it up full volume and skank around the front room singing the lyrics: 'Free-eeee Nelson Mand-e-la.' And we would all join in. Of course, I didn't know who Nelson Mandela was but I loved the jazzy African rhythms.

On a Sunday, Fat Daisy usually showed up just after dinner. Mum always did a roast dinner on a Sunday. Always with chicken. And sometimes she'd make an apple pie, with little leaves on top made from the leftover pastry. Fat Daisy would barge in and head straight to the fridge, looking for the remains of our roast chicken. Like a lion, he'd attack it furiously, tearing and ripping at the bones, trying to remove every last scrap of meat. Then he'd throw the gristly bits of chicken into a large bowl and smother it with salad cream, piccalilli, Tabasco sauce, or whatever the greedy bastard could lay his hands on. He would speedily devour the lot, wrapped in slices of bread. I was secretly glad on the days that Fat Daisy came and ate all our leftovers, though. If he didn't, they would be used to make the dreaded chicken toenail soup. I huffed at my mum on those grim Monday evenings when she served me a bowl of the thin broth with bits of carrot and potato floating in it. It looked like something you might find brewing in a witch's cauldron. Hubble bubble, eye of newt, and all that.

'Eat it up, it's good for you,' my mum would say.

And I'd be slumped there with my head bowed over the bowl. I'd slowly slurp the oily liquid while staring at the telly, the flickering white light and the upbeat theme tune of *Blue Peter* ruining my sulk.

Our TV was rented. It was a big grey box with wooden sides and a curved glass front, and it had a contraption attached to the back. You had to put a fifty pence coin in the slot and turn the lever to make the telly work, and the TV man would come every Wednesday to empty all the coins into a cloth bag. The television frequently turned itself off once the fifty pence ran out and we often didn't have the money to turn it back on. We lived in constant fear of hearing the heavy clunk sound halfway through a programme. Luckily, Fat Daisy knew a magic trick.

I liked magic tricks. I'd seen a real magician over at Marsh House once. He had a top hat and a cape and he shut this older kid inside a wooden box as if it were a coffin. And then the magician hacked the box in half with a long saw and there was all this fake blood squirting out of it. It worried me a bit but I knew the kid would be alright because he was smiling and waggling his feet. Me and Daryl tried to recreate that trick in my back garden with a cardboard box and a rake. I asked my mum for a magic set so that we could put on a show for her but I never got one.

But Fat Daisy's magic didn't feature any wands or silk hankies or anything like that. It involved getting a pair of scissors and popping open the box on the back of the TV so we could get the coins out. Fat Daisy performed a similar stunt with a pin and the gas meter under the stairs. And when the man came around to read the meter, we all played a game called 'carpet swimming', where we had to lie down on the floor and pretend we weren't home.

'Shhh! Keep still,' my mum would whisper as I fidgeted, our noses buried in the stinky, pink shagpile as we waited for the gas man to go away.

I sometimes wondered if other families had to dive behind the sofa when someone from British Gas knocked on the door. Bit exciting, I suppose. But I also got the feeling we might be doing something wrong. I worried about what might happen if the gasman saw us. Would we be in trouble? Would they take my mum away? Would I be left by myself?

Then I'd get to thinking about other things. Horrible scary things, like this bad man called The Fox. I knew The Fox was real because I'd heard people talking about him, saying he was a night prowler who hid inside dustbins, and Little Daryl said he'd seen him in the woods behind our house. They were even talking about it on the telly. They said he was called The Fox because he snuck into people's gardens at night. I don't know if he looked like a fox, though, because he always covered his face up so just his eyes were showing. I think that's why my mum kept a hammer under her bed and why we sometimes had to stay in and shut all the doors and windows, even if it was really hot outside. Because The Fox might creep into our house and hide, then wait patiently for his chance to do us in before slipping away into the night.

Come to think of it, I reckon that's probably when I first noticed that feeling deep in my tummy. The one that kept on telling me everything wasn't okay.

December 2019

It is a Saturday afternoon. I've got the heating on; I can hear the water clanking and sloshing through the pipes. I'm lying on the sofa and watching a film about this blond-haired boy who's been left alone in his home, and he's jumping on the beds and eating ice cream. I've seen it a hundred times. I'm tired because I've not been sleeping well. I'm having nightly dreams. Lucid, disturbing dreams which are set in different places. Sometimes, I'm lost as I travel through some exotic country, trying to find my way home. Or I might be with my family in a car which is speeding out of control through city streets. Other times, I dream that I'm silently wandering through dark corridors. The only common thread, as far as I can see, is that they all feature children: usually my own children or me as a child. I might be in the house I grew up in, or outside, playing with friends. Sometimes, I'm being chased. Often, there's blood and screaming.

At some point in the film, I drift off. I'm woken by blaring music and bells ringing outside. I don't know what time it is but the movie has ended and it's dark now. I shuffle over to the window and part the curtains; the neighbours have got their shitty reindeer lights up. A white truck drives slowly past the house. It's brightly done out like a sleigh and there's a bloke dressed up as Santa Claus squished in an armchair on the back of it.

I'm still groggy and lethargic, so I stretch my legs out on the sofa. I immediately remember the dream I'd just been having. I'd dreamt I was playing out in the street. My friend Little Daryl was there. And there were some kids hanging around on the waste ground nearby, speaking in another language. Daryl and I ignored them and slipped off through a gap in the wire fence and past the bushes which led to the block of flats where he lived. We found ourselves inside the flats, in the kitchen of a man and a woman. The woman was thin and nervous and her husband was taking strange items from the fridge and feeding them to us. Something seemed not right, so I made my way out of the flat, leaving Little Daryl inside.

Next, I was standing outside, looking up at the windows and the balconies. On the side of one of the buildings, there was a plaque with some writing on it that I couldn't make out, but something in my gut told me it said '1987' underneath it. I looked across at the balding patch of grass where the foreign kids had been playing and noticed a wreath of flowers. I went across the grass to investigate to find some toys and letters scattered next to the flowers. The kids were all staring and speaking in their foreign language now. I wondered why they didn't come any closer, and then I realized that the toys and flowers were next to a deep hole which seemed to get narrower towards the bottom. I peered tentatively down the hole and lying there, at the bottom, was the twisted dead body of my friend Little Daryl. I said, 'May you rest in peace', but nothing happened, so then I said, 'and may I find peace here on earth.'

The doorbell rings and jolts me back to reality. I don't answer it. It's probably the Santa brigade. Remembering the dream has made me feel heavy and tense. It's as if there's something stuck inside me that's trying to force its way out. Like when a bit of acidy sick rises into your mouth but you keep trying to push it back down. I decide to have a bath. I don't know why: I hate baths. I think my aversion to bathtubs stems from the fact that we never had a shower when I was a kid, so scungy baths were the only option.

But I feel better after the bath. And I begin to wonder why I've been so tired and stressed and why I've been having all these weird dreams, summoning up grainy images and muffled soundtracks from the past. Is it some sort of crazy psychosis? Am I on the verge of a meltdown? Or maybe it's to do with facing my own mortality. Like a mid-life crisis or something. Some guys grow a ponytail and have it away with a receptionist. I'm having dreams about a dead schoolboy.

Chapter 5
Mutts and Mayhem

Red and yellow custard, snot and bogey pie,
All mixed up with a dead dog's eye.
Stir it all up nice and thick,
And wash it down with a cold cup of sick.

Playground rhyme

'Tell him I'll be out in a minute,' I shouted down to my mum when Daryl flipped the door knocker one sunny weekend morning. I had already rushed up to the bathroom to look for my favourite piece of clothing: my Superman suit. My mum never got around to washing the suit, so I knew if I wanted to wear it, I'd have to root through the wicker basket to find it. I fought through the tangles of damp clothes to get to the blue and red outfit which was buried at the bottom. I couldn't find the cape, so I threw on the top and trousers, all crinkled and smelly, and ran out into the bright sunshine. Daryl was sitting on the edge of the path. He was a tough boy with unruly brown hair which sprouted across his face like a Play-Doh mop top. My friend was crouched in his T-shirt and cut-off jeans, examining a piece of chalk which, just a few moments before, he had been using to scribble noughts and crosses on the kerbstone.

As I approached, Daryl looked up at me and made an impish smile that revealed his missing teeth. Then he whisked the hair out of his eyes and flung his white stone off into the gutter. 'Errr,' he went, wiping his hands down his already soiled T-shirt. 'Yuck!'

I knew straight away what he was on about. The chalk Daryl had been writing with was *actually* a pellet of dried-up dog muck. It was common for us to mistake petrified dog poo for chalk because there were loads of semi-domestic mutts roaming freely around our neighbourhood. Jack Russell's, Doberman pinschers, and everything in between. There was even a three-legged mongrel that used to come down our way. And they'd all be shitting in the street, so of the many varieties of turds which adorned our pavements, some would end up becoming crusty and white with age.

The first thing Daryl and me did was go through the alley to check on our tadpoles. A few weeks earlier, we'd been around the corner to the river, armed with our little nets on bamboo sticks. It wasn't really a river—more of a stream—but we liked to balance across the big metal pipe like tightrope walkers and duck down into the dark, smelly archway under the bridge. You wouldn't've thought there would be any fish living in that murky old river, but there was. And if we waited patiently for the long shafts of sunlight to pierce the brown water, we could spot the spiny minnows and sticklebacks. We didn't catch any, though we did manage to net a few splodges of frogspawn. We lobbed them into a metal bucket and carried it back into my garden and left it by the shed. Daryl would come round every day after school to see them, and we got excited when we saw some wriggling tadpoles emerge.

Now, we were waiting for them to change into frogs, which we knew would happen once they grew their legs and lost their tails. They had already sprouted their little legs but, annoyingly, their squiggly tails were still there. It was taking too long. Me and Daryl were getting impatient, so we decided to give them a helping hand. We scooped the half-froglets out of the water and laid them on the cracked concrete. Then we each took a sharp rock and surgically removed the tails by sawing and hacking at them with the stones. Once the tails were off, we plopped the slimy stubs back into the water but were disappointed to see them sink to the bottom of the bucket.

'How comes they ain't turned into flippin' frogs?'

'Dunno,' said Daryl, shrugging his shoulders.

A load of soapy water came splashing out the end of the drainpipe and we looked up to see my mum's face in the kitchen window. She was doing the washing up, so she wasn't looking at us, but I was worried about what she might do when she found out what we'd done.

'Don't worry,' said Daryl. 'We can just say it was all my idea.'

I felt relieved, and as we came through the alley and back out into the street, I wiped my mucky hands down my Superman shirt. 'What d'you wanna do now? Tag, kerby, cops and robbers, knock-up ginger?'

'Zaki! Zaki!' Daryl called out as he noticed our friend on the other side of the street.

His full name was Zachariah Stewart but we called him Zaki. He was a local hero. All us kids in the street loved Zaki because he always took the time to stop and talk to us. Zaki was a professional boxer and looked it: he was cool and handsome, as tall as a lamppost, and he had these massive muscles which bulged like boulders through his polished purple-ish skin. He seemed old and giant to me, but he was probably only in his late teens. Sometimes, he came across to our house to see me and my mum and he had to duck his head down when he came in through our door. Our dog always growled at Zaki whenever he came over. 'Your dog's vicious!' he'd complain. 'I'll ring the council and have it put down.'

But he was only joking. He knew our dog wasn't dangerous. Boo was just a protective pooch who liked to chase motorbikes and watch over us kids as we played in the street.

Just as Zaki got near to Daryl and me, the ice-cream van came hurtling by, dinging its happy chime. We looked up at Zaki in anticipation and he was sporting a big smile, like the Cheshire Cat from *Alice in Wonderland*.

'Yous want an ice cream, yeah? Go on, then, my treat. Choose what one yous want.'

Normally, we just got what we were given, so me and Daryl took our time deciding what to have. In the end, we both chose a Feast. It was either that or a Cornetto, but we'd had Cornettos before. Besides, the Feast looked like it was the biggest from the pictures on the side of the van and they were normally only for adults. Zaki took the two Feasts from the ice-cream man and tore open the bright blue wrappers. He gave Little Daryl his one first. I think he liked Daryl better than me because he used to talk to him more and Daryl would look him in the face and answer all his questions properly like a grown-up. I reached out for the lolly with my eager little mitts, but Zaki quickly pulled it back.

'What do you say?' I didn't know what he meant so I stared downwards and inspected the white flecks on my fingernails. 'Nice one, Zak' he told me, beaming with his wide smile, showing me what seemed like hundreds of straight white teeth.

I lifted my head and fixed my eyes back on the Feast. It was like a posh choc ice except with knobbly bits. And even though I'd never had one, I knew it had chocolate in the middle. Zaki crouched down and handed it to me, then put a massive hand on my head.

Little Daryl had already slurped down his Feast and had brown sludge all around his mouth. He was reading out the joke on his lolly stick: 'What's yellow and stupid? Thick custard.'

I felt a bit stupid because I didn't really get the joke but Zaki and Daryl were both laughing, so I laughed, too.

After the jolly giant was done telling us that he was a cousin of the famous pop singer Jermaine Stewart, he blinked, making his eyes twinkle in the hot sunshine, and turned towards his house. 'Come on then, boys, I'll show yous something.'

We'd never been in Zak's house but it must've been a Sunday because his mum had gone to church. Zaki's mum was a stern West Indian lady who always wore a scarf on her head and never laughed or smiled.

He opened his front door with a key and led us into the over-furnished front room that was only for guests. I knew no kids ever went in there because it was dark, cool, and smelled old; it was sort of clean and dirty at the same time. The heavy curtains were only half open, and there was a settee which still had the plastic wrapping on it. In front of the chairs, there was a dark wooden table with a dustless surface which gleamed like a mirror around all the lace doilies. We knew we weren't supposed to be in there, which is what made it all the more interesting. Zak pointed us toward the tall, glazed cabinet along the back wall. It contained porcelain dolls dressed in funny costumes, nick-nacks, and glass ornaments, as well as an embroidered map of the Caribbean islands. Those things weren't for playing with, but it didn't matter because we weren't there for that old crap anyway. Our eyes, wide like saucers, were instead drawn up to the shelf displaying Zaki's sparkling boxing trophies. I counted them: fifteen in total. Too many for the one shelf so they were all stacked up like the crown jewels. Zaki was proud to show them to us and we were in awe.

'Nice one, Zak. See ya later, Zak,' Daryl lisped as we stepped back out into the warm white daylight.

Daryl talked with a lisp because of his missing front teeth. He was a happy-scrappy sort of kid who'd talk to anyone and he used to roam all over the neighbourhood. Everyone liked him.

'Oi, Daryl,' I said, tapping him on the shoulder as we were about to cross the road.

'Huh?'

'We're mates, ain't we, Daryl?'

'Yeah, course!' He chuckled, squinting his eyes nearly shut and rocking himself back and forwards like a chubby chicken.

I stopped and stared at the sunbeams glittering off the car windows. And then, I thought about what Daryl had told me about his stepdad doing bad things. 'Yeah, but what if they was—?'

'You're it!' Daryl swiped the hair from his eyes and slapped me across the chest with his fleshy fingers. He had already run across the road and pegged it halfway up the street by the time I realized we were playing tag. I scampered after him. Daryl might've been tougher than me but I was way faster because I knew how to run with my hands flattened out like spears. I easily caught up, but he turned the other way and cut across the gardens, zigzagging between bins, then hopped over hedges to avoid me. He doubled back down towards Zaki's house, leapt across the pathway, and without looking, nimbly slotted his chunky body in between two parked cars.

All I heard of it was a snot-curdling *SCREEEECH!* and then a dull *thunk.*

I spun around quickly in time to see Little Daryl bounce off the front of a blue car like a football. The stretchy-time thing was happening all over again as I inched into the gap between the vehicles. Daryl was lying in the middle of the road, panting like a tired dog. Every time he opened his mouth, he let out a deep howling noise and waves of tears tumbled from his wide eyes. A man got out of the car now and hunched over Little Daryl with his hands on his head. The man looked worried and started saying stuff but I didn't hear any of it because I was too busy gawping at my friend who was lying on the concrete like a leftover Jelly Baby.

Luckily, Zaki must have heard the racket because he came sprinting out of his house and over to us. I took a step back as Zaki bent down and scooped Little Daryl up off the asphalt.

My mind was racing, and I thought about a school assembly where they'd given us a talk on the Green Cross Code. Daryl didn't stop, look, or listen; he'd just darted out into the road. I wished I'd found my cape so I could have swooped down and caught him, like how Superman did when that kid was about to get chopped up by a combine harvester. But I didn't, did I?! Instead, I'd just stood there like a goon in my faded red and blue suit. It was the first time I saw someone get run over.

Zaki was cradling my little friend in his strong arms. Daryl was shaken and bruised but he looked like he'd be alright. He never stopped bawling, though. I watched the man get back in his blue car and drive off, but my memory's blank about what happened next. All I can remember is Zaki coming back to my house a little while later. I was stretched out on the sofa, pretending to be asleep, and I could hear him explaining to my mum about all the noise and the blue car and the driver.

'And he was standing there, yeah?! So I've gone and picked the kid up off the road and I've carried him around the corner.'

'What, to the maisonettes?'

'Yeah, and I'm bangin' on the door, yeah, and he's still crying in me arms like, and it's as if no one's bothered 'cos they ain't answering. But I knew they was in, you know, 'cos I can hear the telly going and all that, right?! Finally, the geezer comes to the door with his missus, yeah, and she's got the asshole 'cos of me banging. So I tell 'em about wot happened and everything, and he's just stood there, glarin'. Next thing, he grabs the kid and shuts the door on me. Know what I mean?'

I desperately wanted to know what he meant, so I shut my eyes even tighter and burrowed my head in the arm of the sofa. I figured Zaki must've been talking about Little Daryl's parents. I mean, I knew he lived with his mum and his stepdad. But weren't they going to take care of him?

Even though we all thought the sun shone out of Zak's ass, I guessed that he probably wasn't an angel. I mean I never saw him do anything bad, but I supposed he might have done because the police used to show up sometimes looking for him. One time, when I was watching TV, I saw his rangy figure hurdle over our gate and fly past the back window. And when I went out the front to see what was going on, I saw that there were two police cars parked up by Zaki's mum's house.

Another time, I saw Zaki from a distance while I was at the park. I was sitting on top of the giant spider climbing frame that made a loud ding when you whacked it. All the paint was peeling off, so the sour metal made your hands stink. Zaki was lumbering down towards the shops when a panda car came down the road and stopped right next to him. Two coppers got out of the car, so we all ran over there to see what was going on, and by the time we got there, Zaki was giving out because one of the Old Bill was trying to put him in handcuffs. The other one was grabbing Zaki's head like it was a bowling ball and, together, they bundled him into the back of the tiny car. By now, a bit of a crowd had formed and we were all getting a bit lively because we didn't know what our mate Zaki was getting arrested for. To be honest, we didn't care. All that mattered was that he was one of us. So, we all crowded around the panda and started pushing and rocking the stupid little police car. We were hoping that we could topple it over, but we couldn't. The panda revved its engine and zinged off around the corner like a Scalextric. It quickly disappeared out of sight with my friend in the back. That was one of the last times I saw Zaki. At some point, I heard he made his way to London.

I sometimes went to London with my mum to visit a lady called Sunie. She was my mum's best friend and they had grown up together. Sunie was small and animated and different from the other people who came around. She smoked skinny French cigarettes and spoke in a way that made you want to listen, like the people on the TV do, using delicious words and flashing the whites of their eyes. She taught us how to say supercalifragilisticexpialidocious.

Sunie had moved to London to work in pop music. I don't know what part of London Sunie's flat was in but, from her window, I could see all these cranes and tall buildings and there was a river with boats on it. Because Sunie worked in the music business, she knew all sorts of famous people. I drooled over a picture of her and Boy George that sat proudly on her dresser.

I always felt a bit tingly about going to London as I sat in the back of the car, peering out of the window at the rows and rows of shops. I supposed I was just excited about being in a new and different place. The hustle and bustle on the city streets represented a sort of freedom where you could do almost anything. It was snowing a bit as all the lights and cars and smoke flew by and I was captivated by all the weird and wonderful sights I saw. An Arab dressed in traditional robes, a man holding a parrot, a dwarf scuttling across the street... I kept an eye out for Zaki, too, but I never saw him.

December 2019

My wife is in the living room watching TV, the kids are in bed, and I'm doing the washing up in the kitchen. I've got my music on and I'm nodding along to the beat, lathering up the plates and placing them onto the rack.

'Fuck's sake!'

I must've been a bit overzealous with the Fairy Liquid because the crystal butter dish has jumped out of my hands and shattered inside the porcelain sink. That butter dish was a family heirloom which had belonged to my grandma—my dad's late mother.

It's like a switch has been flipped and, suddenly, there's a ball of white-hot magma rising from my abdomen. I snap off the rubber gloves, step back from the sink, and take a deep breath but it's already too late—the burning ball in my stomach has already exploded into a full-on meteor shower. The flames are licking up through my body and sparks are pissing out of my earholes. The raucous canned laughter from one of those stupid American sitcoms is mocking me from the other room.

I stride in there and shout at my wife: 'How comes you never do the fucking washing up? Why's it always down to me?' She stays silent and carries on watching the TV. 'Ok, so sitting there watching reruns of *Friends* is more important than supporting me?'

Then she swivels her head like the girl in *The Exorcist* and says, 'Not everything's about supporting you!'

Now she's upset and we're both feeling terrible. As I turn, the childish laughter heckles me one last time as Phoebe calls Joey a lobster. I go upstairs and shut myself in the bedroom. I stand with my back against the door, then slouch down 'til I'm in a crouching position with my arms wrapped tightly around my shins. I don't know why I'm so disproportionately angry. Does it have something to do with my childhood? I rock my head back and smack it off the door a few times. I used to do this a lot when I was a kid.

Chapter 6
The Feeling

In 1986,
The queen pulled down her knicks.
She licked her bum,
And said yum-yum,
It's better than Weetabix.

Playground rhyme

I stayed close to my mum after she had fainted in C&A, following her whenever she went out into the kitchen or the garden. Often, we'd go to a place called Leagrave, or 'up the top' as we called it. I don't know why: it wasn't up high up or anything, except for the steep slope where you could peer over the iron railings and watch the cars going by. It was where our local branch of Kwik Save was and where we got our weekly supply of no-frills groceries and crusty rolls. The rolls often looked a bit dirty but they tasted good when buttered and stuffed with a slab of mouth-tingling cheese and some crisps. To get up the top, we went by the mobile library and The Cement Shed, past the posh bit where my Grandad Ron lived, and through the alley by the Sugar Loaf pub. I'd skip ahead to see the field full of lambs who didn't know they were going to end up in the butcher's across the road. Inevitably, that would make scary thoughts come into my head, so I'd go running back towards my mum and the pushchair. Sometimes, we went to Purley Market with its little indoor shopping precinct or to Dunstable. Other times, we hoofed the four miles to Luton town centre. We walked everywhere: we had no car and no bus money.

Once a fortnight, Mum would cash her giro at the post office. Thirty bob, it was. And we had to stand in the long line with all the coughing, grumbling old gits clutching onto their pocketbooks. After Mum's money got slid under the glass, we'd go to Co-op to get our daily rations where my mum would say hello to Carol who'd be standing in the doorway, next to the big pile of empty cardboard boxes that I always wished I could dive into. It was mainly on the weekends that we went up the top, returning home with plastic bags hanging off the handles of the buggy and stuffed underneath the seat.

There was a garden centre up the top. It was boring and I hated going there but my mum liked to walk along the narrow aisles of plants and talk to Rosa, the Italian lady who worked there. Rosa was small and dumpy, with short black hair and rosy-red cheeks which matched her name. The only good bit about going to the garden centre was the paper shop next door where you could get a ten-pence mix of sweets. The inside of the shop was long and dark and I could smell the piles of newspapers and magazines that flanked the doorway. I studied the shelves lined with chocolate bars and Sherbert Fountains and different coloured paper tubes of Refreshers and Rolos and Fruit Polos. But what I was really interested in was the big plastic tubs behind the counter that contained an assortment of penny sweets: vampire teeth, foam bananas, chocolate saws, tattoo bubble gums, traffic light lollies, and candy necklaces. The owners of the paper shop were a grumpy Indian couple: he was slim and silent and she was about three feet tall and had a red dot on her forehead. I think it vexed the lady how I peered over the counter and spent ages going along the line of plastic containers saying, 'One of those...er...one of those...one of those,' pointing at the flying saucers and foam shrimps. I'd start over again once I had one of each. Then I'd repeat the process for my little sister.

The lady with the red dot would lick her finger to pick up the paper bags and, then, with the same spit-covered fingers, she'd angrily peck at the sweets and thrust them inside. I'd often hear her saying something in another language to her husband, which in my head translated to, 'Why doesn't the little shit just ask for four cola bottles, two shrimps, three saucers, and a candy fucking cigarette?'

On one occasion, after we'd got our sweets, me and Sophie waddled back to the garden centre to look at the goldfish pond. Mum was standing nearby with Rosa, yacking on about the weather and flowers and stuff while we dipped our fingers into our sugary bags and peered down at the little orange flecks darting around in the lilies.

It was at that moment that I first got the feeling that I was going to do something bad and knowing that there was nothing—*nothing*—I could do to stop it. I was watching my little sister like a toad eyeing up a bug when a strange urge or impulse whooshed over me. I knew it was beyond my control: it was boiling up from my feet like a volcano. A build-up of energy where once the idea has formed, there is no going back; an overwhelming sense that I absolutely must follow through. And without any thought for consequence, I thrust out my short arms forwards and launched the bandy-legged baby into the pond. The water wasn't all that deep but it was cold, and I just stood there looking while Sophie floundered like a fish amongst the weeds.

Within seconds, there was panic all around and I got thrown aside. Several adults came running over and Sophie was heaved out of the pond, gasping and dripping with cold green water. It didn't help that she was wearing a fluffy jumpsuit which absorbed the pond liquid like a big sponge. After all the commotion had died down, I got pulled by my wrist and stuffed into a red phone box. I stood there silently, peering out through the cracked glass while my mum used what coins she had to make a series of desperate calls for a lift. No one answered, so I got kicked all the way home.

Sometime after, my new baby brother, Tommy, was born. Little Tommy Tucker we called him and, sometimes, when my mum wasn't around, I'd call him Little Tommy Fucker. Everyone who came around our house adored Tommy. We even made up a song about him: 'Tom-Tom, the pipefitter's son' because his dad, Martin, sometimes worked as a pipefitter. Tommy was a happy, hyperactive child, sparky and agile and full of life. Our mum had her work cut out, though, because Little Tommy Fucker never learned to crawl like most babies and he seemed to skip walking altogether. He was running around the place by the time he was eight months old.

I was in the second year of infant school now, and I hated it from the start. I wish that I could tell of a wonderful smiling teacher who nurtured me through my school years but not a single one of them seemed interested in teaching or my learning anything. Perhaps they took one look at me and decided I wasn't worth their effort. Or maybe I just wasn't interested in learning. I definitely wasn't interested in times tables or dorky spelling tests. Or the way the lessons dragged on unless they involved something like growing cress in a cupboard or making stuff out of pipe cleaners. And I wasn't interested in all the orders and systems and stupid rules. Like putting your hand up to talk and having to keep your books neatly stacked in a stinky plastic folder. But the part of the school day I dreaded the most was lunchtime.

As I came from a single-parent family, I qualified for the category that no child wanted to be in: free dinners. Free dinners might sound like a good thing to some people but it wasn't to us. When the lunch bell rang, me and Daryl would drag our feet down to the dining hall and stand in line with the small number of other shitbags that were on free dinners.

While we waited, I'd enviously eye up the other kids—the ones who actually looked forward to maths and PE lessons because they had calculators and football boots. And at lunchtime, they had plastic lunch boxes which they flipped open to reveal things like Trio bars, neatly packed jam sandwiches, and cartons of UmBongo. Perhaps even a tiny red box of Sun-Maid raisins.

Little Daryl never complained, though. He had a good appetite, and he mostly always ate his dinners up quickly so he could go play in the playground. But just the reek of the hot slop wafting along the corridor made my stomach turn. Just thinking about that lumpy mashed potato, lukewarm beans, and stinky grey matter carelessly slapped onto a plastic tray by the dinner ladies with their massive metal spoons gave me a queasy sinking feeling in my gut. To make matters worse, us 'free dinners' had to sit at a separate table from other kids, too, while the dinner ladies, in their pale lemon tunics, wandered around, checking we had eaten everything before they'd let us go.

It seemed as though a dinner lady's job was to stop children from having fun. But I knew they weren't like real teachers because we were allowed to call them by their first names. One of the dinner ladies was a tall, stringy woman named Ginette. She had a pointy face with brittle-looking hair on top which reminded me of Bacon Frazzles. Ginette used to try to make me eat the fat ugly peas which came in the mixed veg—the disgusting-tasting ones were rock hard, like swollen grey bullets. I devised many tricks to deceive Ginette and her co-workers, like spreading the food out or hiding it in my pockets. But my piece-de-resistance was my mock heaving. I had it down to a fine art. The heaving was partly genuine, as the texture of the insipid mashed potato did make me want to throw up, but I exaggerated it for dramatic effect. I'd tip my head back and rock my chair while shouting, 'Weeuuuuuggggghhhhhh! Weeeeuuuuuggggghhh! Weeeeuuuuuggggghhh!' This would cause a scene and three or four belches would usually suffice to draw the matter to a close and have me sent on my way to the playground.

The school playground was an expanse of cracked grey cement where we noisily chased each other around or huddled in corners trading stuff. Once outside, I'd get my own back on Ginette by heckling her with my special rendition of a song from a TV advert for Gillette razor blades: 'Wooaah! Ginette! The best a man can get.' But Ginette wouldn't say anything. She'd just stare at me with her bug-eyes bulging from her pointy face.

I wanted to be good at school. I knew it was the right thing to do and I knew the answers to most of the questions, but I never liked putting my hand up. I wanted to be like the well-behaved children, with their neat hair and uniforms. I wanted to follow the rules and be quiet and please the teachers, but I couldn't. No amount of gold stars taped to my jumper could make me do it. I wasn't your typical naughty boy. I wasn't rude and I didn't throw tantrums but there was a restlessness bubbling inside me. A kind of curiosity or boredom.

Like when I sent off for the Fingermouse activity sheet. *Fingermouse* was a crappy TV show starring a mouse-shaped finger puppet that played musical instruments. At the end of every programme, they'd show an address where you could post an envelope. And if you wrote your name and address on the back, they would send you a free fun pack with all the stuff to make your own paper mouse. The pack also included a magazine and another boring paper-based game called 'Flap the Kipper'. I don't know when or how, but it occurred to me that they probably didn't keep track of who had applied. So, over a period of months, I posted lots of envelopes and received many Fingermouse 'fun' packs in the post (none of which I either wanted or needed). I felt a tiny bit guilty about inventing this little stunt. But not enough to stop me from repeating the exact same scam with the Dennis the Menace fan club. After all, I knew that this type of crime wouldn't carry any punishment as there were no real victims and my mum wouldn't have worried about a few missing envelopes from the kitchen drawer.

At school, however, things were different as there were rules and teachers whose job it was to enforce them. The first time I got into trouble at school was when a jar of coloured pencils was placed on the table for us to draw with. Little Daryl showed me how easy it was to snap the pencils in half, so I picked one up and broke it with a satisfying click. Little Daryl done one, and then I done another. Snapping those pencil sticks gave me a feeling of power and I liked it. They popped easily, like twigs in the woods. We were like a couple of them rebellious punk rockers. Like that headbanging Johnny Rotten fella who my mum listened to. Me and Daryl got carried away and we must've broken around eight or nine pencils each. Then the teacher saw what we were doing and came over to the table. Mrs Whitelock was an old teacher who wore plain coloured dresses and, yes, she did have a tightly curled dome of pure white hair that made her look a bit like a poodle. She put one hand on her hip like a teapot and swiped away the jar of pencils with the other. Then Mrs Whitelock pulled me by the arm over to her desk and started asking me questions: 'Why did you do it?' and 'Do you know that pencils cost money?'

I said, 'I did' and that 'Daryl had told me to do it'

And Mrs Whitelock responded with, 'Well, would you put your head in an oven if Daryl had told you to?'

I was a bit puzzled by that question, so I didn't answer. Instead, I just looked over at the snazzy pencil sharpener that the teacher had on her desk. It was big and clunky, with a hole where you stuck the pencils in, and it had this windy handle that you had to turn to make it work. I wanted to have had a go but the selfish teacher had told the class that only she could use it. Me and Daryl were made to stand in the corner for the rest of the afternoon. They also sent a letter home to my mum saying she had to pay for all the broken pencils.

When I got home, I stuck out my bottom lip and told my mum I was sorry. I tried to show her that I really meant it because I'd once heard my mum telling my dad that she was dirt poor and never had a pot to piss in. I expected her to get angry and smack me but, to my surprise, she didn't. Instead, she hugged me and said that I shouldn't have broken the pencils but not to worry because they didn't cost much anyway.

The following week, my mum received another letter home and, this time, it was accompanied by a phone call from the school welfare officer. It had to do with something which had happened on the weekend. I'd been over at my dad's house, and I was sitting with him watching the telly while he was busy strapping up one of his zoots. Emrys carried around this little pocketknife which he used for cutting up his gummy blocks of hash. It had a short, curved blade which folded down into a wooden handle with gold patterns on it. As any young boy would be, I was curious about the neat little folding contraption with its sleek steel shank. I'd always wanted a penknife, so I asked my dad if he'd let me hold it. He wouldn't but he did snap the knife open and start clowning around with it, saying he was going to chop my willy off. My dad was laughing and I could tell from his actions that it was a game. But it still made me a bit nervous, so I leapt up and ran into the narrow kitchenette. My dad followed, playfully waving the shiv towards me. I knew he wasn't about to slice off my wang but I panicked and flung my hand in the direction of the blade, making contact with the glinting silver arc and slightly nicking the outside edge of my right thumb.

This was typical of Emrys' parenting style: always trying his best to be funny and different but often getting it wrong. Like the time he attempted to teach me about the birds and the bees. I returned home to my mum with talk of orgasms and a hand-sketched diagram of a clitoris. The thing is, I reckon he just wanted to teach me the things that he thought were important.

Back at school on Monday, I was standing next to the teacher's desk again, smelling her pukey perfume and reading from a book about some stupid boy called Ben and his dog, Lad. I had to match up the three-letter words on the page with the small cardboard cutouts which were kept inside a tobacco tin. I was busily sorting the cards on the desk when the teacher noticed the gash on my thumb. 'How did you do that?' the teacher asked, taking my ham-coloured hand, and turning it over.

'Er...my dad was trying to cut my willy off.'

Then the teacher told me to pack up my reading stuff and made me go and see the school nurse. The nurse didn't even really look at the cut; she just kept on asking questions and writing stuff down, and then she gave me a brown envelope and sent me back to class. The following day, my mum had to attend a meeting at the school where she attempted to explain away my dad's unique brand of horseplay.

January 2020

It's a gloomy winter evening and I'm sitting at my desk with my MacBook and a cup of tea. I'm tapping away at the keyboard but I don't just feel like just a middle-aged man writing down some silly childhood stories. I also feel like a six-year-old kid who's getting a kicking for pushing his sister in the pond.

I'm still the same person as when I was a kid, with many of the same thoughts and sensations. Of course, I no longer feel the physical pain of a good hiding I received many years ago but thinking about it still elicits the same sense of shame and anger. And when I remember back to the day in C&A when I thought my mum had died, it is now no more than a dusty little card in the filing cabinet of my mind, but it's still there, catalogued under the label 'Most Scared Ever Felt'.

As an adult, I carry many of the same beliefs, emotions, and awarenesses. Like those moments of foresight, anticipation, or instinct when I saw things right before they happened. They are fewer and farther apart now but I still have them.

I've heard people talking about clairvoyants or superstitions or premonitions or whatever. But this is more like a subliminal text or a wireless energy signal which puts me into a sort of trance and tunes me into the right frequency to receive the information. I used to have these moments a lot when I was a kid. It can be something good or bad, big or small. It's as if I'm momentarily pulled out of my skin so I'm looking at myself from above, then an invisible man taps me on the shoulder and goes, 'Pssst, hey, bucko. Just a quick heads-up. Some shit is about to go down and you have *zero* choice in the matter. It's non-negotiable.'

Like the time I was given the number 74 ticket in the school raffle. When I stuffed the pink cardboard coupon into my pocket, I just knew it was a winner. I felt it. I didn't know I'd win a voucher for a perm and blow-dry at Richard Anthony's hair salon up the top, but that's not the point. (I gave it to Colette from next door.)

And like the other time, when I was standing at the top of the stairs at home. I was about five years old and I had this sense that I was about to fall. I even envisioned my runty little figure twisting and tumbling over the carpeted steps. And sure enough, even though I was aware it was going to happen, there was absolutely fuck all I could do to stop it.

It's like how I've always known that I was going to write about all this stuff. One day.

Chapter 7
Chips and Videos

There was an old man named Martin Finnegan.
He grew whiskers on his chin-a-gen.
The wind came out and blew them in again.
Poor old Martin Finnegan.
Begin again.

My version of the 'Michael Finnegan' nursery rhyme

It didn't matter that he was clean-shaven; it still brought me great joy to sing this song to Martin Finnegan. He didn't like me singing that song. He didn't like a lot of things. Martin was Sophie and Tommy's dad, and my stepdad, I suppose, even though I didn't want one. He'd said I could call him Dad if I liked but I preferred not to. Martin lived with us, although he wasn't always there. I knew when he *was* there because I could smell the burnt toast he liked having for breakfast. When I smelt it, I stayed out of the way.

He'd been born in Ireland but moved to London with his family when he was a boy. That's what he said, anyhow, but it might not have been true. I don't think he was a bullshitter; he just knew a lot of things and he liked telling stories. He liked drinking, also. And swearing. Martin was definitely Irish, though, and I think stories are sometimes more important than the facts for the Irish. You could see this in how he would answer a question. It could never be yes or no. Rather, it'd start with, 'I once knew this fella named Gerry, and Gerry had a wife...'

Martin had this deep, dopey voice that made him sound a bit like the cartoon character Deputy Dawg. But he wasn't dopey at all; he was clever and he knew about all sorts of things. He was handsome, too, and I liked how his Feargal Sharkey hair swished like a curtain over his nut-coloured eyes. Martin smelled like car engines and, sometimes, he and my mum did French snogging on the sofa. It looked disgusting how they'd rub their mouths together and squirm around. I kept to myself whenever I saw them doing that.

I invented secret nicknames for my stepdad like Moody Martin and Martin Always Fartin'. Fat Davey called him Hitler because of his sketchy little moustache. He and Fat Davey were best mates (even if Martin didn't like the nickname). They'd both grown up on the next estate and they liked going around drinking together. Fat Davey was the leader of their gang.

Martin had good taste in music, too. He mostly listened to Elvis Presley and Buddy Holly, but he also liked country and western. One day, Martin brought home this small record in a paper sleeve. We all sat on the sofa, listening to the scratchy recording which sounded all jangly and twangy. Some drunk bloke was wailing in a silly voice, yowling, and carrying on like a hurt dog: 'Goodbye, Joe, me gotta go. Me-oh-my-oooh.'

But Martin loved it. He was happy, then, waggling his knees and tapping his foot while trying to sing along: 'Jambalaya, crawfish pie and file gumbo-oooh-oooh. Sonofagun, we'll have some fun on the bayou.' I didn't know what any of those words meant but I was tickled silly.

It was hard to know if it was to do with his drinking or if Martin was just forgetful, but it seemed as though he always liked to start things and not finish them. He'd got married when he was sixteen and, when that didn't work out, he became a soldier, though he ran away from the army because they found something naughty in his locker. The army caught hold of Moody Martin and stuck him in prison but he didn't like it when this was mentioned. After his short army career, Martin worked on building sites as a pipefitter and, after that, he spent some time working in a place called the Middle East. I had always been interested in new and different places, so I asked him what it had been like.

'It's hot and it's hard work. But it's also fun because you get to go around catching lizards and helping build sets for *The Raiders of The Lost Ark*.'

Martin loved kids—he had two sons from his previous marriage who sometimes came over to play—and he'd often pile us all into his van and take us places. When he was feeling happy, me and Martin played a game called 'pushing lions', where we got down on our hands and knees and bumped our heads together. He taught me how to shine my Doc Martens to a hard mirror gloss with his little wooden-handled brush. 'In the army, you have to polish your boots every day, so they stay waterproof,' he said. ''Cos the tops are made out of leather, see, and the bottoms are from old tyres.'

I suppose Martin was a sort of father figure to me but I was constantly reminded of the fact that he wasn't my dad. The reminders came in the way that he used to swing between playful and annoyed, like the pendulum of an old person's clock. His moods puzzled me. My mum said Martin was the type of man who goes a bit funny when they don't have routine and discipline. One time, Martin took me to the barbers to get a crew cut. I enjoyed sitting on the bench with him, waiting for my turn, eyeing the barber man as he held a wide comb on top of the boys' heads and then buzzed over it with the electric shears to get a perfectly flat top. But when we got back home, Martin poked me in the chest and shouted at me for using too much of his hair gel: 'How many times have I gotta fuckin' tell you, eh?' I wasn't sure of the answer, so I just kept my head down.

He owned a leather belt with metal spikes on it, too. He threatened me a few times with the spikey strap, though I never experienced the sting of it and nor did Martin ever smack me. A few thick ears and the occasional dig, but that was about it. Like the time I was spying on him in the bath. I was listening to Michael Jackson on my Walkman and I could see the outline of his naked body through the crack in the door. As if he knew I was there, spying, he spun around in the bathtub and shouted across the landing, 'Oi, turn that fuckin' shite down, will ya?! I fuckin' 'ate that Michael Jackson.' Then he came out of the bathroom with a towel around his waist, called me a turkey boy, and clouted me around the back of the head, sending my headphones crashing to the floor.

It made me uneasy whenever Martin did things like that. But while he could be moody, I knew he wasn't a bad man. I think he just liked having things a certain way.

Martin had a younger brother called Barry. Barry Finnegan had a runtish look about him: he was small, like a jockey, with googly eyes and milky white skin. Mum's friend Sunie said that he looked like a freckle on a stick. Barry had an incomplete tattoo of a naked lady on his gangly forearm. He had other faded tattoos on his hands, too, but it was the naked lady one I found the most interesting. It was a fuzzy blue-green colour and the girl had only one wonky tit. When I asked him why it wasn't finished, he said that he'd done the tattoo himself but it hurt too much, so he gave up halfway through. I figured that Barry must've been forgetful like his brother.

Martin and Barry knew how to have fun with us kids. They used to take me and Little Daryl to the park and, occasionally, to the fair. In the summer, we picked blackberries and, once, when it snowed, we went sledging. Sometimes, when my mum had one of her headaches, Martin and Barry would take us to the chalkpits behind the big Tesco. Or to Marsh House. The walk to Marsh House was down the alley and then under the railway bridge and through the woods. The same woods where Daryl said he'd seen The Fox, but I tried not to think about that. I loved bulldozing through the muddy trails, crunching twigs and kicking up the damp leaf litter as I went. At the end of the woods, there was this foul-smelling pond that marked the source of the River Lea. We called it the Bog of Eternal Stench after the film *Labyrinth*.

'That's where Boris the Bog Monster lives,' Martin said, trying to scare us.

The putrid pond was polluted with all sorts of dangers and nasties. There were the usual food wrappers and empty drinks cans but, also, motorbike parts and upturned shopping trollies which looked like ancient weed-covered dragons peering up out of the water. A bit further down, at the part where the pond joined with the river, there was this massive tree that had a burnt-out hole in the trunk. Me and Daryl loved to climb inside the belly of the tree which Martin said had been struck by lightning. 'That's why the trunk's all black and hollowed out,' he told us.

The tree's thick arms leaned out over the river and one of the arms had a rope swing hanging off it. We took turns to dangle from a knot on the frayed blue twine and make Tarzan noises as we swung out over the water. If you were skilful enough and you timed it right, you could jump off and land on the other side. But if you missed the jump, you might end up bouncing back and forth. Or in the water. That's what happened to Barry. He wrapped the rope around his broomstick body and, just as he was about to jump, he lost his footing, slid downwards, and got his foot stuck in the sinking mud. We called that a booty.

'Shit! I've got a booty,' Barry yelled as he tried to pull his shoe out of the brown goop.

The oily river snaked its way up and around the back of Marsh House via a hidden nature reserve.

'All this used to be an old burial site,' Martin said, pointing at the grassy knolls across the way.

'How old?

'Well, old.'

'What, like, in olden times?'

'Yep.'

'Older than Baby Jesus?'

'Yep.'

'Even older than the dinosaurs?'

'Yep, we're walking over pre-historic graves. Except, now, it's called Waulud's Bank. Bet yous din't know that, did ya?'

'No.'

'Well, yous do now.'

Waulud's Bank was a quiet, peaceful place where tree branches dipped in the water and electric blue dragonflies danced around the reeds. And no Fox nor bog monster in sight. Daryl and me would run on ahead, following the trail which became a wilderness, and we'd creep along, trying to catch a glimpse of the moorhens and water voles which nestled on the grassy banks before we emerged back out at Marsh House.

Even though you could get to it through this sort of riverside secret garden, Marsh House wasn't a secret. Everyone knew about it because it was this humongous brick building with a swirling psychedelic mural on the side. Most importantly, though, it was where the adventure playground was. The adventure playground was a place of wonder; where kids came from all over the town to climb on the rickety wooden structures. And they'd always return home with injuries from all the nails and splinters which protruded from the old faded planks. They had decent swings there, too, and a death slide. And there were these log bridges and ladders which led up to lookout towers. Me and Daryl used to climb up the turrets so we could spy on the kids below. And at the centre of the playground, there was a massive wooden maze which had a series of dark tunnels. I enjoyed crawling through those cramped, damp passageways and watching the flecks of dust twinkling in the shafts of sunlight which pierced through the cracks in the wood. But Martin didn't like me going in there because he reckoned it was full of strange people.

'Full of funny fuckers in there,' he said. 'Right funny fuckers.'

Another time, when Martin's Always Fartin' was looking after us, we were watching one of those live telethon shows. Terry Wogan was presenting it and while I wasn't interested in the appeals to help the poorly African kids, I was all pumped up by the music and all the different comedy sketches. Celebrities were being gunged and I was impressed by this mystic man who could bend spoons with his mind. I went into the kitchen and got a spoon to see if I could do it. But I couldn't, so I put on a hat and started acting the goat instead, mimicking the silly catchphrases I'd learned off the telly: 'Now then, now then, how's about that, then?' Good game, good game, and let's see what you could've won.' I even did my Lenny Henry routine, but everyone stayed glued to the screen. Tough crowd. They'd seen it a hundred times before.

Then I remembered this kid from school who had shown me this thing called 'the spastic walk'. I'd asked my mum what a spastic was and she told me that I shouldn't say it because it was a nasty thing to call someone who was handicapped. But it couldn't be that bad because there was a shop called The Spastics Society where Mum used to go to get her flowery shirts and jeans, plus the kids in the street used to say spastic all the time. They even bulged out their bottom lips and shortened it to 'spaccy' or 'spaz'.

Since my mum wasn't there, I decided to try out the walk. Surely, this would win over my audience.

I was wrong. I did a couple of laps of the front room, stumbling and dribbling, until Martin clamped a hold of my twitching arm and squeezed it really hard.

'Oi, fuckin' pack it in!'

It was around this time that Martin tried to make his own beer. He had all these big glass bottles in the house which he told me were called Lady Janes or demijohns or something. But he must have forgotten to finish his beer-making because one of those Johns, Janes, or demi-jars ended up filled with coins in the corner of the living room. Martin told me to tip the jar over and count all the pennies inside it. He said that once I had counted them all, we were going to give them to the poorly children in Africa. I poured the coins all over the floor and carefully placed the coppers and silvers together in little piles while Martin was on the phone to Terry Wogan. After that, he made me go upstairs and collect all the toys that I didn't play with anymore. I reluctantly brought down my battered Action Man figures and put them with the pile of coins for the poorly African kids.

I'd once heard my mum telling Colette next door that Martin's job was spasmodic. I asked her if it had anything to do with the handicapped but she said it just meant that he preferred drinking beer to going to work. But Martin must have been working when he brought home the video player. It arrived in a big box which Martin said had come off the back of a lorry. The video player was grey and futuristic-looking, with a top-loading mechanism that raised up slowly like the doors on a DeLorean. Watching videos was way better than normal TV, except we always had to rewind the tape after we'd finished because the videos had to be returned the next day.

Friday was chips-and-videos night at our house: Martin said it was because we shouldn't eat meat on a Friday, so we had to have fish instead...but we couldn't afford fish, so we just had the chips. We would get a mountain of fat yellow chips wrapped in greasy white paper for fifty pence. And after going in the chippy, we'd go next door to the video shop, where we would spend ages looking at all the posters and cardboard cutouts, and the covers of all the action and horror films which were lined up along the dusty shelves. Once we got home, the chip bag would be torn open and dropped in the middle of the floor and we'd peck away at the glistening chips like chickens eating corn, never taking our eyes off the screen.

We weren't allowed to watch the really scary movies but Martin would bring home pirate videos. They were never about pirates at all, but they didn't have covers and the picture went a bit funny sometimes, so we'd have to fix it by spinning a little wheel on the underside of the recorder. One time, Martin brought home a film about some boys who were walking on the train tracks because they wanted to go see a kid's dead body. It worried me a bit because I'd never seen a dead body before, especially not a kid's. And the boys in the film were being naughty and getting into trouble. I never knew if they got to see the dead kid, though, because the clunking sound happened and the TV switched off halfway through the film. Martin started cursing, then, and bounced his knee up and down as he fumbled around with the little black film canister that he kept his dope in, rattling it and banging it on the table. He lit a fag and went in the kitchen where he started going on about a stitch-up and a dosshouse as he slammed the cupboards again. After a while, he walked back out into the hall, combed his Feargal Sharkey hair, and pocketed the comb. 'That's it, I'm off down the fuckin' pub.'

The next morning, Little Daryl came and called for me and we bounced our way to school like a couple of bear cubs. I told Daryl about Martin and the film with the boys going to see a dead body. 'Glad I never seen the ending, though,' I said, looking down at my scuffed school shoes.

'What you on about?'

'Bit scary, ain't it?! Walking on the train tracks and all that? Mind you, them boys didn't look all that scared.'

'Durr!' Daryl responded instantly. 'Prob'ly 'cos they was mates. And mates stick together, they look out for each other.'

I figured Daryl was probably right—if it was us, we wouldn't have been scared, either—so I relaxed a little and the two of us started mucking about, just like the boys in the film, as we dawdled past a decrepit old house. It had a concrete path that led to a front door with peeling brown paint. On either side of the path, there was a long, overgrown front garden which was home to a humongous horse-chestnut tree. The leaves were orange and the heavy conkers were already starting to fall. We turned to look at each other and our eyes lit up.

Conkers were like crack to us, second only to football stickers. We played a game where we'd have to choose a conker each and jook a hole through the middle of it with a nail. Then, we'd thread a shoelace through the hole and take turns to try and smash each other's conker. If you won, your conker would become a one-er, then a two-er, and so on. I don't know what number you had to get to but, if you kept on winning, eventually your conker would be crowned a grandad. Daryl told me that a conker with a flat edge was called a cheese-cutter and he taught me all the rules like tangles and stampsies, as well as how to harden your conker by putting it in the oven or soaking it in vinegar. Once, we lugged a bag full of conkers to school and threw the lot in the playground. 'Scrambles!' is what you shout when you chuck something on the floor (usually money) and then watch all the other boys as they go tumbling after it.

It must have been early in the season when me and Daryl spotted that giant tree in front of the old house. Neither of us had any conkers yet, so seeing that conker tree was like a godsend. Normally, we'd throw a stick up to knock the spiky green shells down, then we would have to stamp on the rubbery husks and pry the swollen conkers out by hand. But this time, we were in luck because they were already scattered over the ground, waiting for us.

And there were loads of them, as if they were being served on a plate. We hungrily rummaged through the overgrown weeds, trying to locate the shiny globes. I could see Daryl stuffing them into the pockets of his grey school trousers when, out of the corner of my eye, I noticed that the paint-blistered front door of the house was halfway open. I raised my head. That was when I clocked the doddery old geezer standing there. He had long bushy sideburns and was wearing a dirty green coat with patches on the shoulders. He was holding something long and thin by his side. Then I saw that half of the old man's face was grimacing as he slowly raised the object towards his bristly cheek. It looked like a cricket bat or a funny-shaped stick...but not. That's when I realized he was holding a gun. I'd never seen a gun before, not in real life, but I knew that's what it was. It had a wooden handle and a long metal barrel and it was pointing right at us. Daryl must've seen it, too, but he didn't say anything. There was no time to speak or even think. Just... Turn! Duck! Run!

Everything was moving really fast but it felt all long and stretchy, like chewing gum. Me and Daryl rubber-legged it down the hill towards the big iron gates and we fell into the playground, trembling, our lungs burning. We raced straight into the classroom to tell the teacher what had happened and, by the afternoon, word had got around about the incident. Everyone was asking us questions and my mum even came to meet us after school. We walked a different way home and Mum walked Daryl and me to school the next morning, too.

'That's the one,' I whispered when the old house came into sight.

The knot in my stomach tightened as we tiptoed past the path. I tried to keep looking straight ahead but something caught my attention. I couldn't resist looking downwards and, to my surprise, someone had placed a box at the foot of the path. It was an old shoebox with the words 'help yourself' scrawled on the side. It was filled with glistening reddish-brown conkers of all shapes and sizes.

We didn't dare lay a finger on them.

PART 2

THE TERROR

Chapter 8
Forever Seven

What do policemen do with their puddings?
They put them in custard-y.

Joke told in my youth

It was around six months later when I heard Martin say those three terrifying words: 'Little Daryl's dead.' It'd made me feel all wobbly like jelly and as hard as stone both at the same time. I just couldn't comprehend it. I mean, I knew of people who'd died on our estate before. My mum had this friend who'd been hit by a train while taking a shortcut across the tracks behind our house. My mum was supposed to have gone with them, but she'd changed her mind last minute.

I'd heard about this other kid who'd lived in the flats. He'd been killed when he'd stuck one of his mum's hairpins in a plug socket. That's why

I knew to never go near them. My mum's constant warnings made sure I steered well clear of hairpins *and* plug sockets.

And there was this other lady my mum knew. Her name was Avril Dunn. Her beaten body had been found in the woods a year before. Everyone seemed to know about that because they were going on about this thing called a manhunt. It was supposed to be a way to search for the murderer but they never found him. Not until years later when they invented a thing called DNA.

But these were all *other* people I'd heard about but didn't really know. Little Daryl was *my* friend, *my* classmate, *my* little pal. No one had ever explained to me about death or dying, so I had to try to figure it out for myself. I tried to ask questions but I received no answers. I listened out for clues, occasionally overhearing words like 'murdered' and 'killed'. And so, instead, I became a private investigator, observing the adults and earwigging on their conversations. I did my best to piece together snippets of information but the adults were being tight-lipped.

And then I saw something. Something that would add fuel to my fear and confusion. It must have been a Saturday morning because it was just after I had finished watching *Sesame Street* and the adverts were on. I was sitting on the floor with my back against the pale green sofa when I looked up from my bowl of Sugar Puffs and I saw a picture of Little Daryl on the screen. I was startled to see him there and it made me a bit dizzy. He was wearing his knitted jumper, his face was chubby, and his shaggy hair looked like a helmet that was too big for his head. I tried to pick out the words that they were saying:

'Killing...stepdad...charge...'

A sickly mix of terror and misery forced its way down my tight throat. And I got that weird sensation again: when I couldn't move but everything else was collapsing around me.

'Luton...police...custard-y... Body...butcher...knife.'

The whizzing in my brain got worse and it made it hard for me to take in the sounds and pictures that were coming from the TV. And my tummy was all twisty, as if I was hungry but not hungry. I pulled my knees up tightly towards my chest and I shut my eyes. And then I heard them say, 'Michael...Fish...weather...'

I remember wishing I could understand more about what had happened so it would make sense to me. I wanted to go to Daryl's home to try to find out for myself. To search around for anything suspicious, like fingerprints or a scrap of clothes or spots of blood on the pavement. But I guess I was kept in. Besides, it was mid-winter and I was seven years old.

That following week, I had to go back to school and it started with an assembly. Assemblies were where all the kids had to sit cross-legged in rows on the cold, brightly varnished floor. It wasn't fair because the teachers got to sit on chairs along the sides of the hall and some kids didn't even have to go to assembly because they were Jehovah's Witnesses. We had to sit through the headmistress telling stupid stories about clever spiders and good Samaritans. But sometimes, instead of the stories, a special guest would talk to us about fire safety or stranger danger. Like the time a man came and did tricks with a yo-yo and, afterwards, everyone got a free one with Coca-Cola written on it. But even on those occasions, we always had to sing hymns. ('He's got the whole world in his hands. He's got the whole wide world in his hands...') I didn't mind the hymns that much but as we went into assemblies, we had to line up and each boy had to hold hands with a girl. This could be a problem if you got put with someone you didn't like. But I usually ended up with a pretty girl called Heidi Metcalfe because her last name started with an M, same as mine.

As we filed in, I noticed a long word written in big letters on the board: 'Tchaikovsky'. And there was soothing ballerina music playing over the crackly speakers. I knew what the word was and that the song was called 'The Nutcracker' because we'd been learning about it before Christmas. The gentle headmistress standing at the front of the hall was called Mrs Seamark. She was thin, with wispy gold and silver hair that was cut short like a skullcap. Mrs Seamark spoke softly, saying a prayer for Little Daryl. We sang a hymn, then the headmistress told us that Little Daryl had gone to heaven.

After school, I asked my mum again what had happened to him.

'I don't know, love. There's loads of rumours goin' 'round.' Zoe pursed her lips as she went back into the kitchen.

I could see my mum's face through the hatch; she was rubbing around her eyes like she had a headache or something. Then she gave me a mug of milky tea and a Wagon Wheel—the ones with the jam in the middle.

Maybe my mum knew more than she was letting on. Perhaps she hoped it would go away and I'd forget about it. But kids are smarter than that. Zoe was right about one thing: there were a lot of rumours, cooked up by the wild-eyed gossips in the post office queue, claiming that the boy's stepfather was a psycho who'd strangled him in his bed. A lady who lived in the flats said the whole family had been poisoned and stabbed to death. Another nosey neighbour reckoned that a madman had done the kid in, wrapped him in a sheet, and carried him through the streets and down to the police station. All sorts of frightened whispers were floating around the school playground, too, about night prowlers and 'polterghosts' and the infamous Freddy Krueger. And even though my mum never let me watch any of the Freddy Krueger movies, I knew what he looked like. But this wasn't a movie, it was real.

I didn't know what had happened to Daryl but I knew it was bad and that it might've involved his stepdad. I thought about it a lot. I conjured up gruesome images of blood, lots of blood. And I often pictured Little Daryl's still-waxy corpse: his pale face with a fat purple tongue poking out; his body, all bleached and bloated, like how ET looked when they pulled him out of the water. These thoughts occupied my mind day and night, and they scared me. They wove their way into my dreams, bad dreams, nightmares where I was dressed in my Superman suit although not flying but falling, plunging, plummeting through the air towards the hard concrete. I tried to bury those thoughts in the back of my head as the school year advanced but they kept on coming back. I felt like I needed to know what terrible thing had happened to my friend. I especially needed to know if it *was* his stepdad who had done him in. I needed to know if that was what stepdads do.

January 2020

All my life, I have been plagued by the mystery of what happened to Little Daryl. It bothers me that, for thirty-three years, I've felt him scratching away in the back of my mind. It bothered me when I was seven and it bothers me now. Every so often, I see that same image of him. As clear as day. The ghost child staring at me from the TV screen. Imploring me to remember.

I've asked questions but no one knows anything. I have searched countless times on the internet, using various techniques and resources, but I've discovered nothing. I've flicked and scrolled through endless pages of search results and I'm astonished that there is no reference to the events which have disturbed me for three decades. Is it possible that the death of a child can be so forgotten, so lost in time, so unimportant?

No, I don't believe it can be. So, amidst the dull winter light, a slight drizzle in the air, I stride towards Central Library with my wife and kids. I spring up the stairs with a sense of determination that I'll unearth some evidence that will uncover the mystery. I spend a couple of hours filtering through the files and newspaper microfilms.

Nothing.

It doesn't make sense! It had been on the TV, so I was certain that some scraps in the old yellowing articles must exist to hold up some clues. But nothing. Not even a morsel of information.

And then it dawns on me that, without any facts, I am looking for a needle in a haystack.

My eyelids are heavy. My family is waiting for me downstairs in the children's library. They are getting impatient, so I decide to call it a day. I feel confused and disappointed. After all this searching and finding absolutely nothing, I am starting to doubt myself. *Did Daryl exist? Was he an apparition? A figment of my imagination? A long-lost imaginary friend? A phantom of the mind? A sympathetic spectre I'd conjured up to help me cope with my own experiences.*

Chapter 9

Keith's Brother's Got a Plastic Arm

Jesus Christ, superstar,
Came down from Heaven on a Yamaha.
Done a skid,
Killed a kid,
Crushed his balls on a dustbin lid.

Playground rhyme

Things weren't looking good. My little friend was dead and I was struggling to make sense of it all. I was confused and didn't know what to do. I didn't know if I'd find any new friends to play with. And I really didn't know if I'd be safe, whether the grown-ups were gonna look out for me, or if I'd have to start figuring out life all on my own.

During the winter months, I always seemed to have dry lips and a runny nose. Mum said I had a weak chest, so she bought me a parka jacket off the market. She couldn't afford a fashionable snorkel one with orange lining, so mine was an oversized blue anorak with a bit of scraggy fur around the hood. She also made sure I always had my stripy *Dr Who* scarf wrapped tightly around my neck and that I never left the house without my balaclava. It wasn't the full-faced bank robber type but it *was* hand-knitted...like the scarf. And it was plain grey, with a round opening which framed my face like I was looking out of a hole in the side of a ship.

Heavy snow fell that winter. They called it the Big Freeze of 1987. The school had to close for a few days and by the time we went back, all that was left were piles of grey slush heaped around the edges of the playground. The cold concrete was glazed over like an iced bun, but that didn't stop me from having fun. I ran around blowing jets of steam from my mouth, slipping and landing on my ass, only to jump up and do it again. But I got bored with skidding around on my own. I wanted someone else to play with.

There were a couple of goody gumdrop girls in my class, Charlotte Green and Katie Cooper. They were the OHP monitors, which meant they were responsible for setting up the overhead projector for assemblies and for switching the wibbly acetates in between the hymns. Charlotte and Katie were the kind of pupils who could be trusted *not* to make rude hand signals in front of the lightbox or to take a note along to another teacher without reading it. The type of squeaky-clean girlies who had neat handwriting and rolled their eyes and probably said things like 'Takes one to know one'. Girls with pencil cases and tidy bedrooms and whose parents would have encouraged them to stay away from a snotty scumbag like me.

I didn't have a lot of experience with females. Sure, I had a little sister and there was the odd tomboy in the street who sometimes showed us her fanny. But I was too scared to play with the pretty popular girls. And, of course, I couldn't admit to actually *wanting* to play with them anyway: that might have classified me as a sissy or a softy.

All I *really* wanted was for them to notice me, so I cooked up a sneaky plan. I decided that I'd be able to get close to the girls if I allowed them to give me a snow bath. And it worked. The girls seemed to revel in bossing me around and rubbing dirty snow into my balaclava, and I loved the attention.

But when the two girls got bored and buggered off to play hopscotch, I was left on my own again, with chattering teeth and a soggy scalp. As I squinted across the playground to where the two girls were playing hopscotch, a warm bead of mucus slid onto my crusty top lip, leaving a peppery tingle in its wake. And I realized this must have been how Lofty must've felt on *EastEnders* when Michelle Fowler left him standing in the church on their wedding day. I stood there thinking about that for a minute, then I blotted the sticky string of snot away with my cuff and slithered off to tell the teacher that I was wet and cold because of what the girls had done to me. Charlotte Green and Katie Cooper got made to apologize to me and they had to spend the rest of the week's playtimes indoors. The next day, there was fresh snow and as I played in it, I could see their miserable faces glaring scornfully at me through the window of the assembly hall.

The hall had a shiny floor and ladders which folded out from the walls. There were also strange gym apparatuses with leather tops which the teacher said were called horses. We never got to go on them, though, but I didn't care because they were rubbish-looking horses anyway. The hall was used mainly for assemblies but, every Wednesday, we went in there to do a thing called country dancing. It was an ordeal which involved skipping around in your pants and vest while a teacher in a red cardigan clunked away on the upright piano. The teacher in the red cardigan was called Miss Miller and she told us that the reason we were doing country dancing was as a sort of audition for the annual maypole festivities. Naturally, the OHP monitors were chosen to partake in the maypole event and, for some reason, I was also selected. Miss Miller explained to us that the maypole is an old English tradition where a wooden pole is erected in a field in early May. She showed us how we would have to skip around the pole while holding the coloured ribbons attached to the top.

'It's similar to Morris dancing,' the teacher continued, 'which is another ancient folkloric dance practised in rural regions of the country.'

It didn't sound good. And it brought to mind something I'd seen on TV where these old white men were waving handkerchiefs and frolicking around to fairy folk songs at some sort of boring jamboree.

The teacher enthusiastically informed us that this year's harvest festival was being held in a nearby village called Caddington and that it would be attended by Bob Monkhouse from *Opportunity Knocks*. The teachers and the other children seemed excited about it but I wasn't a fan of Bob Monkhouse and the idea of maypole dancing had me worried from the start. Despite my nervousness, I did my best to join in, but when the elastic waistband snapped on my baggy blue Y-fronts halfway through the first practice, I wanted out. Me and a few other boys were being instructed on how to pick up the nylon ribbons and then hop over to pass them on to a girl. The problem was that every time I bent down to pick up a ribbon, the cheap pants flopped open and my tiny willy shot out like the bird in a cuckoo clock.

I decided that I would try to survive the first segment of dancing and, once it had finished, I'd go over and tell Miss Miller that I wasn't feeling well, hoping she would allow me to sit out the rest of the practice. As soon as the music stopped, I jogged on over towards Miss Miller with my hand in the air, then I skidded to a halt in front of her.

CUCKOO!

The young teacher's gormless smile dropped as I fumbled to poke my pale prick back into its polyester pouch. Having my pecker pop out for the teacher to see was an excruciatingly embarrassing experience for me.

But it did get me excused from doing any more of that stupid maypole dancing.

***

When the school holidays finally arrived, they seemed to last forever. Six whole weeks of long balmy days playing out in the street until dusk. But like in school, with Daryl gone, I didn't have many other kids to play with, so I ended up knocking about with these two brothers who lived up the nicer end of the street. Patrick and Brendon, they were called. They might have been twins, I'm not sure. They were a bit older than me and went to a Catholic school. Brendon had short black hair in a bowl cut and Patrick was taller with mossy brown hair that looked like a bird's nest. They showed me how to jump the river—you had to jump a bit further out because the edges were made of sinking mud—and they taught me to play football in the dead-end around the corner. We were playing there once when I realized that I needed a shit badly.

'That's alright. No need to go home,' Brendon replied

'Yea, just do it over there in the bushes,' said the other one.

I went over to a patch of bright green weeds, pulled down my shorts, and did a long, mushy crap. But I hadn't thought it through to the next part. I looked around for something to wipe myself with and spotted a packet within arm's reach amongst the dock leaves. It was faded yellow, and it had KP Skips written on it. I grabbed it and rubbed my backside with the prickly packet but it just made even more mess. I started to panic and, as I tried to pull my shorts up, I ended up skidding over the steaming pile that I'd just laid. Patrick and Brendon started cackling and pointing and I felt a scalding humiliation as I ran home plastered in my own poop. My mum was furious. She barked orders at me as she crouched me in the stained bathtub and sprayed me with the rubber hose attachment. 'Stand up...sit down...turn around.'

'But...but—'

'But what? Look at the soddin' state of yer!'

'But the bigger boys told me to do it,' I said, shivering and whimpering.

Our street joined with another street called Hookers Way. Little Daryl's maisonettes were on Hookers Way. I don't know why they were called maisonettes. Daryl said it was a posh French word for a house. I'd never been to France and neither had Daryl but I believed him because he knew about things like that. Even though the maisonettes didn't look very posh, or French. They didn't even look like houses. Next to the maisonettes, there was a block of dingy garages which I used to use as a shortcut. Most of the garages didn't have doors and there were tatty cars, broken TVs, and soggy mattresses dotted around. I swear people lived in those garage blocks. A dog called Karl the Old Station lived there. I asked my mum why he was called that.

'It's not old station, it's Alsatian. They use them as police dogs.' She said it with a smile but I still thought Old Station sounded better, especially if they used them at the police station. 'And that one is called Karl, same as you.'

Karl the Old Station might have had the same name as me but I never liked him. Not one bit. He reminded me of the Big Bad Wolf: his manky grey fur was all covered in bald patches, and he was cunning, too, because every time our dog was in heat, he used to come to our house and flip the door knocker with his long-pointed muzzle. Normally, if I saw a mean-looking dog in the street, I'd just bend over and pretend to pick up a stone and it would usually make them go away. But not Karl the Old Station. He was too smart and mean for all that. Going for a stone would just make him even meaner and, so, he was the only local dog I didn't trust.

I didn't trust his owner, Nathan, neither. Nathan was a hard older kid who had cheesy yellow hair and wore a tartan budgie jacket. I guessed he must've lived in the flats but he spent most of his time on the streets and hanging around the lockups. Nathan wasn't like the other kids on our street. He was sort of feral and, as far as I knew, he didn't go to school.

Whenever I went through the block, Nathan and his dog would be lurking there, up to no good. And he'd suddenly appear out of one of the cave-like openings and kick me in the shins for fun or yank my clothes 'til I fell over. If I spotted him first, Nathan would smile and beckon me over, all friendly-like. Then, as I walked toward him, he'd start lobbing stones and trying to set his dog on me. On the days that I couldn't see Nathan and Karl the Old Station hanging around the garages, I'd try to run the gauntlet. But after bumping into them a few times, I decided it was best just to take the long way around.

Most of the boys in our neighbourhood were tough, so it was important to know how to fight—or at least to look like I knew. I didn't want anyone to think I was a wimp, so if I met a boy I didn't know, I tried to ask him three things: what team he supported (Luton); who he thought was the hardest in his school; and what trainers he had. I'd then demonstrate my hardness by tilting my head forward and doing my best screwface (a way someone tries to look menacing by pursing their lips and squinting their eyes a bit).

I had my first proper scrap when I was seven. I was at the park with Patrick and Brendon; they were kicking a ball around on the grass, but I couldn't get a touch, so I went over to the rubbly play area. There was this tubby kid I knew from school called Dean Campbell sitting on one of the swings. He was looking at me, doing something funny with his eyebrows. And he had this oval-shaped body that reminded me of a Mr Potato Head. I could see he was bigger than me but that didn't matter because hardness is measured by age, not size. I didn't like him looking at me all funny, so I said, 'Oi, wot yer lookin at?'

'Nuffink, ain't got a label,' said the boy.

That was a good one that was, so I thought for a moment and then I called him Fatso.

And then he goes, 'Shut yer face, Dumbo.'

So I said, 'Get stuffed!'

Then he went and called me Mr Spock and he stretched his ears out and blew a raspberry at me.

I felt stupid and wished I would've called him something good like Mr Potato Head or Humpty Dumpty or something. But it was too late because the boy was already off the swing and walking away. I went over and told the bigger boys what happened and they said I should have a scrap with him.

I didn't want to. I'd never fought before and the thought of it made my legs wobble and my asshole flap. But the boy came barrelling towards us. He'd gone and fetched his big sister who was about twelve and looked like Desperate Dan.

'You comin', Fresh?' said the sister.

'Nah, I'm comin' stale,' I replied smugly.

Then the sister looked at Patrick and Brendon. 'Oi, dis fuckin' kid's well facety,' she went, jerking a thumb towards me.

The tubby boy had on his bottle-green school jumper which rode up over his belly. His fists were bunched by his sides like clubs and his cheeks were all flushed.

The fight went on for what seemed like three weeks but, really, it probably wasn't longer than three minutes. It was mostly just a wild flash of scratching, hair-pulling, and slapping. I breathed in the boy's hot sour odour as I gripped onto the fleshy rolls at the sides of his body. And when he started heaving and prying at my face with his clammy little palms, I kneed him in the chest. I'd heard that the best way to win a fight was to kick them in the nuts, so I tried that, but the boy kept on getting too close and our legs got tangled up. The next thing I knew, we'd both fallen over and were rolling around on the grass. The bigger kids stood nearby on a dusty mound, hooting and hollering. I think we must have got too tired to continue, or maybe we just forgot why we were fighting, because we eventually separated and pulled ourselves up off the dry turf. Dean Campbell ran away and sat on the bridge, sweaty and sobbing, to be consoled by his big sister. I was glad I never had to fight her instead; I bet she knew how to have a scrap.

On the plus side, Patrick and Brendon seemed to like me better after the fight. They included me in their games, let me kick the ball, and even gave me a bunk up onto the garage roofs.

A week or so later, we were playing a game called runouts. It's an upgraded version of hide and seek, where you find your hiding place but then you have to try to run to a certain spot, like a tree or a lamppost, before you get tagged. Runouts is usually open to all the kids in the neighbourhood but they must've all been grounded on this particular day because it was just me, Patrick, and Brendon. The gnarly crab-apple tree at the end of my garden was the spot that we had to try to get to and although I had earned *some* credit with the older boys, I still had to go first at seeking. I faced the tree and started counting.

'One...two...three...,' I said, covering my eyes, unaware that Patrick and Brendon had crept up behind me, 'four...five...six...'

I felt one of the boys grab me tightly, so I opened my eyes to find the other one was wrapping a long skipping rope around my waist. Once I realized what was going on, I didn't fight or resist; I just watched as my arms were held in place and they wound the red and white rope around them like tendrils on a giant triffid plant. The two brothers worked quickly and silently, securing me tightly to the tree with professional-looking knots. And then they left. It was a bit like the games I'd played with Fat Daisy, except that this was way easier since I didn't have an eighteen-stone yardie on my back urging me to say, 'Mercy, mercy, Uncle Percy'. Instead, I just felt an inexplicable kind of stillness. I stayed there, all calm and quiet, for ages, listening to the mild breeze whispering through the branches and the birds tweeting in the tree overhead. I looked around, admiring the greenness of our garden, thinking about whether the two lads were trying to hurt me or do me in. And I remembered back to that film where the boys were going to see a dead kid, and they were all sticking together and looking out for each other. I got to thinking about what I'd seen on the news: *'Body…butcher…knife.'* And picturing what a dead kid might look like.

Luckily, before the panic could truly set in, my mum came out to hang some washing and spotted me. She ran over, untied the knotted skipping rope, and gently inspected my thin limbs for signs of injury. 'Why didn't you call for me?' my mum asked, lifting me and kissing me on the cheek.

'Dunno.' I wiped the kiss off my face. 'I didn't want to.'

It was towards the end of the summer holidays when I went back to the park with Patrick and Brendon. I still played out with the two brothers but I tried to keep my distance from them, so I stayed over on the squeaky roundabout. I was lying on my back, looking up at the sky, imagining shapes in the clouds which moved quickly overhead. It seemed like they were all racing off somewhere and I wondered why they could be in such a hurry. Martin knew about a lot of things and he'd once told me that the white puffy clouds were called cumulus and the long scribbly ones were stratus. There was another type of cloud called a cirrus but he didn't say what they looked like.

Patrick, the more confident of the two brothers, was showing off by the swing set. He had flung the swings so violently that the chains were all wrapped up around the crossways bar, then he'd climbed up there to try to untangle them but, instead, he was hanging from the bar, swinging back and forth like a circus gymnast. I knew he was there, but I was doing my best to ignore him. Then I heard a noise like a big slap, so I spun my head around and saw Patrick lying on the ground. I guessed that he must have lost his grip on the bar and fallen to the floor because he was shouting and swearing and rocking from side to side like a fish. I went over there and saw that Patrick's leg was bending the wrong way, as if it were double-jointed. There was this oily shadow oozing through his jeans. It was dark red like Ribena.

'Aaaaggghhhhh! Fuuuuccccckkkk! Shiiitt! Shiiiittt!'

Brendon ran over to the shops to phone for an ambulance, leaving me standing there by myself to watch Patrick as he rocked and cursed like a madman. A steady stream of tears slid from his eyes as they whipped from side to side looking for signs of help. It took a little while for the ambulance to arrive but when they did, it drove right up onto the grass. I craned my neck as one of the men pulled a big pair of scissors from a bag, then watched on in anticipation as he cut away at Patrick's jeans to reveal a twisted, bloody leg.

The ambulance men worked fast. They soon bandaged up the injured leg and then stuck it in a big orange boot. After that, they carefully lifted Patrick onto a stretcher before driving away with both the boys in the back of the ambulance. A scrap of Patrick's jeans was left behind on the floor. *They were his best jeans*, I thought to myself as I stared at the strip of bloody denim fluttering gently in the wind. And then, I just turned around and walked home. I didn't see them two brothers for the rest of the summer, or hardly at all after that. They sort of just drifted away.

I found other kids to play with, though. There was this flabby boy called Keith Nash who had sandy hair that formed a triangle on the front of his head. And he had these things called adenoids which made him talk funny; he kept them in a jar next to his bed. As a result, he sometimes called me Tarl instead of Carl, so I started calling him Teith for a laugh, but I don't think he got the joke.

Keith lived in a pokey flat with his mum and his elf-like little brother. He had a stepdad, too, and, by the sounds of it, he was the wrong kind of stepdad: the kind that I'd pictured in my mind so many times. Keith's stepdad would turn up drunk every Friday night and fight their mum. And if she locked the door, he would stay outside shouting 'til they had to call the police. Keith would always come and call for me the next morning and tell me about it. Sometimes I went over to play at his house, but I only ever saw the stepdad once. He came out of the bedroom in his underpants and I saw he had a pot belly and dark bristles which sprouted from his vest and up to his face. He told us we had to go and play outside, so we took Keith's Ghostbusters torch and took turns shining it up into the dirty stairwells of the flats. I was over there another time when Keith's mum gave him a little glass jar of crab paste for his lunch. I think it was meant to be spread on bread but he didn't have any. I watched him eat the whole thing, scooping out all the fishy mush with his fat finger.

Keith Nash was a bedwetter which meant he had a peculiar smell: a tangy cabbagey sort of smell. His little brother smelled the same, but he also wore pointy glasses with Sellotape on them and spoke with a squeaky voice. I don't recall the brother's name but I do remember that he had a plastic arm. It was beige and had felt-tip marks all down it, like a sleeve of grubby tattoos. I say the arm was plastic—it could've been made of fibreglass or something else but it was definitely solid. I knew how hard it was because Keith's brother was an affectionate child and, sometimes, he would come running over for a hug and he'd accidentally clonk me with his prosthesis.

One afternoon, the two boys were over at our house, playing a game we called bompty-bomp. It's a game which is played by *all* kids, where you slide down the stairs on your ass. I think Keith Nash and his brother liked coming to our house because they lived in a flat which didn't have any stairs. And we were having a good time, too, 'til the one-armed kid ruined it by falling on his head. He might have been put off balance by his clunky arm but us not having any bannisters probably didn't help. Martin had sawn them off the year before. He said he was doing the house up and he was going to build some nice new bannisters with spindles and everything. He must have forgotten, though, because there was just a big gap where the handrail used to be. The kid quickly got off the floor but did so while making this horrible high-pitched screeching noise like one of those annoying party blowers. 'Eeeeeeeee...! Eeeeeeeee...! Eeeeeeeee...!' And he kept on doing that until my mum called a taxi to take him to the hospital.

Later that year, there was a big storm. They said on the telly that it was going to be one of the worst ones we'd ever had and everyone had to stay inside. Sure enough, there was thunder and lightning and big dark clouds. They didn't look like the stratus and the cumulus ones that Martin had described, so I asked him what kind of clouds they were.

He rubbed his forehead and looked down at me. 'Huh?' he said in his Deputy Dawg voice, shrugging. 'D'*you* know what kind of clouds they are?'

'No.' I shook my head from side to side.

'Well, then,' he jeered, 'they're fuckin' rain clouds, ain't they.'

I wanted to give Martin another chance so waited a bit, and then I asked him what made thunder.

'It's because God's getting angry, and he's giving the clouds a good leatherin'.' Martin seemed pleased with this answer but I knew it wasn't true.

I wasn't exactly sure what a good leatherin' was, so I just pictured a big, bearded God up in the sky showing the clouds how to shine their Doc Martens to a hard mirror gloss. I didn't want to ask any more questions because I sensed that Martin might have been getting angry, too. Instead, I peeled back the net curtains and watched the leaves skittering in the wind through the window, the fat raindrops slapping and sliding down the glass.

When God finally stopped being angry and the raindrops got thinner, Martin held my hand and took me around the corner to see what damage had been done by the storm. I saw Karl the Old Station skulking off into the garages. Broken branches and other things littered the road. Martin reckoned the river behind our house had burst its banks, so we went to have a look. Sure enough, the stream had swollen up over the bridge and I imagined myself trying to jump it and getting swept away by the bubbling brown water. That worried me a bit and made me not want to stay outside, so I tugged on Martin's hand and asked him to take me back indoors.

I was also worried about my wobbly tooth which had been hanging on by a thread. I'd been waiting nearly a week for it to fall out. Fat Daisy had offered to attach a piece of string to my wobbly tooth and tie it to the door, so I was relieved when the tooth finally fell out on its own and rattled into the sink while I was brushing my teeth. Fortunately, I managed to grab it before it disappeared down the plughole.

That night, when my mum came to tuck me in, she produced an empty matchbox from her back pocket and held it in front of me.

'Wha's that for?' I enquired, wrinkling up my forehead.

'Tooth fairy.'

At seven years old, I no longer believed in the tooth fairy, but I wasn't about to lose out on the cash, so I played along. 'So, how's she gonna get in here, then?'

'Tooth fairies are only little so they can just fly in through the keyhole and get under your pillow,' my mum explained. But I knew she was making it up because my room didn't even have a keyhole. Zoe slid back the lid of the matchbox just enough to reveal the cotton wool bed which she had made inside. 'Pop your little peggy in there,' she went, and then she kissed me on the forehead and gently slipped the sealed matchbox under my pillow.

The next morning, I awoke with a crust of dry dribble pasting my face to my pillow. I immediately reached underneath it and was pleased to find that the tooth fairy had paid up. Inside the matchbox, resting on the cotton wool where the tooth had been, she had generously deposited a few shiny silver coins. I turned them over a couple of times in my hand and then put them back and stuffed the matchbox under the pillow for safekeeping.

That same morning, Keith Nash came and called for me. The great big storm had been and gone but it was still a bit drizzly, so we played indoors with my Eagle-Eye Action Man and the muscly He-Man figures. My two favourites were a spring-loaded guy called Ram-Man and another bright green moustachioed one called Man-At-Arms. They were boys' toys, and God help anyone who dared to call them dolls. We sat on my bedroom floor and I proudly showed Keith my keyring collection which I kept in my pants drawer. I had a dozen or so of these shiny treasures which had been gifted to me by various visitors and relatives. They were all looped together by little silver chain links and I had loads of different designs. My favourite one had tiny buttons that made the noises of gunfire, sirens, and bombs dropping. I'd been given it by my Grandad Emrys. Another one was blue and it said 'Pepe Jeans' in curly writing. Martin had given me that one because Pepe Jeans were the ones he sometimes sold on the market.

By now it had stopped raining and the sun was poking around the edges of the empty rain clouds. Me and Keith were drawn to the window by the chime of the ice-cream van jangling down the street.

'I'm Popeye the sailor man. I live in a caravan. I like to go swimming and chase all the women. I'm Popeye the sailor man. *Toot-toot.*'

'Come on, Tarl!' Keith giggled as we ran downstairs and skipped outside into the golden-dappled sunlight, our noses filling with that lovely earthy steam that rises off the pavement after it's rained. There was no rainbow, though.

'I've got some pocket money.' Keith fished into his trousers and pulled out a fistful of coins.

The good thing about the ice-cream van was that it didn't only sell ice creams. You could get anything off there: crisps, cigarettes, a bottle of pop. Keith got himself a cornet, a can of Coke, and a pack of cheese and onion crisps, and he treated me to a mini milk.

'Nice one, Keith,' I beamed. I'd learned that line from Zaki.

Later that evening, when I was putting on my pyjamas, I stuck my hand under my pillow. My heart sank when I realized my matchbox was empty. I looked in my pants drawer and found that my keyrings had vanished, too. *But why?* I felt bamboozled. I kept it to myself, though. I was too embarrassed and I couldn't understand why I had been the victim of a crime. Why people were always doing bad things, even to little kids. I climbed up onto my bed and nutted the wall, then I lobbed the matchbox across the room and plugged the tip of my tongue into the little gap where my tooth had been. I cupped my hands over my eyes and cheeks and thought back to that film again: the one where the boys were going to see a dead body. And I thought about all the stuff Little Daryl had told me. About conkers and maisonettes and stepdads. And how mates 'stick together' and 'look out for each other'.

Chapter 10

Running in the Family

Dear Santa,

For Christmas this year, I would like an apple, an orange, and a pair of small Ears.

Carl Meek, aged 7

The same winter that I heard the news about Little Daryl, I wrote this letter to Father Christmas, though my mum never got around to posting it. She stuffed it in a drawer and forgot about it. In the ensuing years, we occasionally pulled it out and had a laugh. For all I know, it's still there amongst the old postcards, bits of broken jewellery, and dogeared school reports.

My mum did her best to keep a tidy house and she always seemed to be busy doing something: ironing, peeling potatoes, weeding the garden, or on her hands and knees, washing the kitchen floor. Zoe had lots of friends but she was certainly a single parent. Me, Sophie, and Tommy never received a penny from our dads, so our mum had to be industrious. She hustled all winter to make Christmas special for us. It was a happy time. She built the joy and anticipation by singing festive songs and we'd all dance and goof about like imbeciles. At the beginning of December, Mum would bring the fat, mildewed box down from the loft. It contained various lengths of raggedy red tinsel, like the stuff they had in the window of the Chinese takeaway. We had loads of plastic baubles, too, and a bird's nest of multicoloured fairy lights which we carefully untangled and draped on the tree—always a real one, and always the fattest one they had at Rosa's Garden Centre. We stuck hand-made paper chains across the ceiling and we taped our Christmas cards to the doors.

Mum always made extra effort to get us through Christmas. And like all good mothers, Zoe went without. From around mid-September, she'd be grafting, working evenings and weekends, cleaning offices, or helping at the markets. She'd take whatever work she could get and do the jobs for peanuts. But that little bit of extra cash meant we could see out the end of the year in relative comfort.

A week before the big day, we'd get the Hoppanstopper minibus down to the big Tesco where I'd ride on the back of the trolley as it rolled past the aisles containing our usual economy brands and we'd pile it high with all sorts of extravagant luxuries. Like nuts, black forest gateau, and dates that came in a long box with a stick. And a tin of chocolates which only lasted about two days. The old ladies on the bus home gave us funny looks when we hauled the shopping bags containing all our festive bounty up onto the luggage rack. Of course, of everything we bought, the most coveted purchase was the telly magazine which, when we got it home, we would eagerly go through, circling all the things we wanted to watch.

The very first Christmas I can remember was the one when Band Aid brought out the song 'Do They Know It's Christmas?' And on Christmas Eve, me and Sophie had a bath and we cosied down next to our mum in our new pyjamas to watch *The Snowman*.

When I woke up the next morning, I went straight over to Sophie in her cot. I was five and she was two. She wasn't old enough to know about Christmas properly, so I unwrapped a present for her. It was a grey bear which she named Graham. I got a Beano annual and a keyboard which played 'Last Christmas' on repeat. Later, we pulled Christmas crackers and wore the paper crowns. And Mum prepared a banquet of roast turkey and all the trimmings: parsnips, Brussels sprouts, and little sausages wrapped in bacon. Even a Christmas cake with icing and little plastic snowmen on top. And we had a starter, too: prawns and lettuce leaves stuffed into a wine glass and smothered in a tangy pink sauce.

One of the good things about having separated parents is that you have two Christmases. One on 25 December and another on Boxing Day. And that means double the presents. I would go to my dad's late on the 26th and he'd have a stocking there waiting for me. It would be stuffed with silly toys from the joke shop: a false nose and moustache, a plastic turd, a fake stick of gum which would snap your finger. One year, my dad surprised me with a pack of nude playing cards. I'm forty now and I still have those things ratholed away in the Kodak box along with my swimming certificates and a badge from the Dennis the Menace fan club. They're not in there because I'm waiting for the opportune moment to dress up in disguise or to play a devious prank on someone but because they mean a lot to me.

One year, I delved deep into my Christmas stocking and pulled out a horseshoe-shaped magnet. It was red with silver tips, like the ones you see in cartoons. It came in a little bag with a string of safety pins stuck to it. A magnet may sound like a strange present for an eight-year-old but I guess it was one of those educational types of toys, like a chemistry set or a magnifying glass. The kind of things which are meant for teaching kids about science. For doing experiments and that but which could also be used for getting up to mischief. Me and Keith Nash were playing with the magnet in the back garden one afternoon. We were using it to pick up toy soldiers and dented matchbox cars, transferring them onto the back of a truck and dropping them down in the dirt as if we were in charge of a miniature junkyard. But we eventually got bored, so I stuffed the magnet back in my pocket so we could go to climb the crab-apple tree. Keith the Thief was climbing in front of me, his backside right up in my face, when I suddenly got an idea. The familiar evil urge came over me and I reached into my pocket and pulled out the string of shiny safety pins which had come with the magnet. I carefully unclipped one and aimed the pointy end at Keith Nash's bum.

'Yoooooowww!' he yelped just like in the *Tom and Jerry* as I slid the pin deep into his meaty buttocks. He dropped down from his branch and hopped home crying.

When my stepdad found out what I did, he told me off and confiscated the magnet and the pins. I knew where Martin hid them but I wasn't about to go and get them. With all the bad thoughts buzzing around my brain, I was nervous about meddling with my moody stepdad and I avoided doing anything that might piss him off. I was constantly worried about what might be coming for me, especially at night, so I always slept with the covers pulled up over my head.

At the time, I shared my bedroom with Sophie. She was in a cot by the door and I had a little bed pushed up against the wall. I'd make a tiny hole in the covers to breathe out of as we sometimes listened to story tapes to lull us off to sleep. It was mainly at these times, when lying in bed at night, that I would get this half-dreamlike sensation. It often came accompanied by dizziness and weird hallucinations, though I'd mostly sense it rather than see it: a strange distortion of space and time, where everything would move slowly. Objects or parts of my body seemed to float around while growing or shrinking. Like when Alice drank the potion before heading into Wonderland. My limbs and fingers would either feel ridiculously thin, like paper, or swollen and super heavy. Sometimes, the sensation lasted a few minutes; sometimes, it seemed to go on forever. It frightened me but I never told anyone about it. I thought I wouldn't be able to explain it or that they wouldn't believe me, so I'd just lie there and wait for it to go away. Hiding in a hot bundle, doing my best to focus on the muffled sound of downstairs voices and the gentle throb of the music, trying not to watch the blades of light crawling across the ceiling while imagining what lurked beyond the curtains: funny fuckers and child snatchers and Freddy Kruegers and all that.

I was starting to get used to being scared all the time but nothing could have prepared me for what happened on the terrible night when I was blasted awake.

THUD-THUD-THUD-THUD-THUD-THUD-THUD-THUD!

Eight measured thuds. I remember it clearly. I was eight.

FUUUUCCCCKKK!

A rush of raw terror was thundering through my chest as I stared into the darkness. There was a stabbing panic in my gut and feverish flashes were spinning through my head. *What the...? Is this it? Am I about to get done in?* I kept completely still and waited for the moment I believed my life was going to end. But then, I was relieved to see the shadow of my mum flapping into my bedroom. Dressed in her green dressing gown, she peered through the net curtains, then she reached forward and popped open the metal-framed window. A slice of light hit my wall.

'Oi!' my mum shouted, closing the window and ducking her head almost simultaneously. I swallowed a gulp of the outside air which had swooshed into the room before burying myself under the bedclothes again, hoping it would stifle the noise and transport me somewhere else.

For a moment, there was silence where all I could hear was my heart pumping the fear and my breath rushing in and out of my lungs as I breathed into the dark. And then there was another set of eight.

THUD-THUD-THUD-THUD-THUD-THUD-THUD-THUD!

'Police! Open up!'

It was pitch dark as I trembled in my duvet den. There was lots of moving around and whispering inside the house. I tentatively poked my head out of my womb-like enclosure. 'What's going on?' I asked.

'Shh,' Mum said, 'it's just next door, go back to sleep.'

JUST NEXT DOOR? SLEEP? Fat chance. I wasn't going to sleep. I was scared sick.

The dull hammering in counts of eight continued for some time and escalated into banging and shouting and screaming, followed by the slamming of doors and the stomping of heavy boots. Eventually, the noise calmed down and all I could hear was the crackling of radios and moans of vehicles reversing around the corner. And after that, just the sound of birds tweeting and the gentle clack-clack song of the trains taking people off to London or wherever. The trembling tightness was still there in my stomach as I winched one eye open for a final check. *Well, I suppose this is just how life is going to be from now on.* I pulled the covers tighter over my head and finally fell to sleep just as it was getting light.

I was awoken again not long after by the whirr and clink of the milk float and I got up to get dressed for school. But I didn't feel tired. Instead, I had a swell of anxious energy. I couldn't wait to ask the kids in the street if they knew what had happened. Prying open the door, I sniffed the air. No burnt toast. Good. And as I whispered down the stairs, I was surprised to hear my mum talking softly into the red phone that was on the table by the door. She was never on the phone that early in the morning. I sat on the bottom step so I could eavesdrop on her conversation.

'Her next door got raided last night... Uh-huh, on the run. Her fella and his mate escaped from the nick and she's only gone and had 'em hiding in the soddin' house.

'I seen someone shining a torch in the camper, so I shouted out the window. Then a meat wagon full of Old Bill comes 'round the corner, so I shut it quick...'

'What? Yeah, stashed behind the radiator.'

I'd been in the house next door many times. My mum used to pop over and drink tea with the lady who lived there. Sophie played with their son, Jared. It was Jared's dad who had escaped from jail and been recaptured by the police that night. I knew it because I spent the following days sniffing around, earwigging, and looking in the newspaper. This time, I was determined not to let any kind of news pass me by.

***

My dad lived on the next estate, Lewsey Farm. He was meant to pick me up every Saturday at 11 a.m. to take me to his parent's house which was also nearby. I'd get up early and zap around the house, eagerly awaiting his arrival. But he was always late. After the Saturday morning cartoons finished, I'd sit through *Grandstand*—the theme tune of which is burnt into my brain. My mum would have me already bathed and dressed and in clean clothes, my hair brushed, and I'd jump up during the ad breaks to peer out of the window to see if he'd arrived.

One Saturday afternoon, I got bored of watching Des Lynam and moseyed out into the back garden. Music echoed out of a tinny radio by the kitchen window: 'Running in the family'. I thought the song was about some kid running away from his horrible family but I enjoyed the punchy beat and the groovy bass guitar riffs, so I did a strange kind of dance while poking around in the remains of the bonfire. It might have been November, although it could have been any time of year; we often had bonfires because there was always stuff to burn. Usually, old items of furniture were reduced to rusty springs and blackened bits of wood. I got carried away and picked up a bit of charcoal which I rubbed on my face to look like Rambo. When I trudged back inside the house, my mum told me off and roughly cleaned my face with spit and tissue.

I returned to the pale green patched-up sofa, listening to the whiny Formula One engines on the TV. I got up and pressed the button to see what was on the other side but it was just some boring black-and-white film. I dived back onto the sofa and spun around, kicking my legs up the back of the chair so my head was almost touching the floor. I liked the feeling of being upside down, all the blood rushing to my head.

And then, just when I'd about given up, I heard a beep outside. I climbed off the sofa, kissed my mum goodbye, and ran outside toward my dad's beat-up old van. My dad never worked after leaving his job as a hospital porter but, for some reason, he always had work vans. This one was mostly white but it had a loose headlamp and one of the doors was a different colour. Emrys flung open the back and I clambered up onto the mattress which was covered in dog hair and empty chocolate wrappers.

I liked going to Grandma and Grandad's house where they always had the heating on full and I'd camp on the floor amongst the fug, half-watching TV and half-listening to the adults while they chain-smoked and argued about the poll tax.

'I don't care if they send me to ruddy jail, I'm still not paying it,' Grandma wheezed. I thought it was funny how she always said ruddy instead of bloody.

And no one told me off for playing with the brass ornaments which lived in the nooks in the stone fireplace. I felt alright there, as if I was somehow far away from all the fears and dangers and all the things that were going on on my estate.

On this visit, I followed Grandma into her greasy kitchen where she'd make salmon sandwiches for everyone. The butter was always kept in the crystal dish on the side and the tea was in a pot with a cosy to keep it warm. Grandma used a fork to mash the tinned fish in a bowl with vinegar, then she pressed the sandwiches down with her three fingers, leaving little dents in the bread. The sandwiches were passed carefully through the hatch (they had a hatch, as well) and we devoured the lot, washing it all down with the sweet hot tea.

After we'd finished eating, Grandad used his walking stick to change the channel over so I could watch my favourite show.

> In 1972, a crack commando unit was sent to prison by a military court for a crime they didn't commit. These men promptly escaped from a maximum-security stockade to the Los Angeles underground. Today, still wanted by the government, they survive as soldiers of fortune. If you have a problem, if no one else can help, and if you can find them, maybe you can hire The A-Team...

The tea swilled and glugged in my gut as I jerked my hips to the military-rock theme tune. I felt embarrassed and I looked around to see if anyone had noticed but they hadn't. So, I leaned on my elbows with my hands under my chin, peaceful and contented, enjoying a rare moment of calm as I stared upwards at a show about tough guys and helicopters and slow-motion explosions.

February 2020

It's raining outside and I'm still feeling flat, so I've decided to spend the morning at home. I'm half-watching some live debate on TV. Students and pensioners are getting worked up about the royal family and Brexit and the state of the economy. And I'm thinking, how is this news? Why aren't they arguing about real stuff and real people? Don't they care? Don't we matter? At the end of the programme, some lady mentions a girl who was raped and killed in a London Park, adding that, on average, two murders are reported in the capital per week. And I realize that it's not that they don't care; it's just that real stuff happens to real people every day. And often, their stories are merely mentioned, with many going untold entirely. If they're lucky, their experience will appear as statistics, slopped into the bottomless bucket of everyday tragedies.

Perhaps I'm guilty of the same. It's been thirty-odd years since I've properly thought about Little Daryl and half the people in this book. Sure, things would pop into my head now and then, but I always pushed them away. But now that I'm giving them more attention, their grainy pictures skip and stutter through my mind like short movies. Old fuzzy films with scenes and soundtracks and characters jittering along. Except they're not actors on a stage or screen, are they?! They're real people. Real people with real stories that have helped shape our world. My world. I believe it's time to get to the bottom of some of these stories, sort through and splice them together, to try to build a clearer picture of what has been and what is yet to come.

Chapter 11
The French Connection

And the Lord said unto Moses,
All the Meeks shall have big noses.
And Moses said unto him: Come forth...
But he came fifth and he lost his bag of chips.

Emrys Meek Sr.

When I was ten, there was another death. And even though this time it was a bit gentler, and it was an old person, it still made me afraid. Grandad Emrys popped his clogs on New Year's Eve, 1990. It was a sad day; the first time I saw my dad cry and I've been unable to partake in a jolly recital of 'Auld Lang Syne' ever since. My dad loved his father, who had been a wonderful example of a hardworking and dedicated family man.

Grandad Emrys was born sixty-seven years earlier in a Welsh mining village called Penrhiwceiber (pronounced pen-receiver) which, according to Wikipedia, is nestled beneath green mountainsides in the picturesque Cynon Valley. The area has recently been named as the most deprived in Wales and it wasn't much different when Grandad lived there. Back then, the predominantly Welsh-speaking community earned their meagre living by working in the coal mines. Grandad and his brothers came from a long line of colliers going back several hundred years and they were permanently smothered in coal dust from being down the pits. By the turn of the century, South Wales had become the largest producer of coal in the world. Men and boys came from all over the country to risk their lives by venturing into the dark narrow tunnels which were carved deep in the Welsh hills. A coal miner's life was hard and they worked long hours to bring out the black gold which powered the homes and factories of the Industrial Revolution. Working underground was a dangerous profession, with an average of one death every six hours due to collapses, explosions, and noxious gases. After the First World War, conditions worsened and, due to the economic decline, the work in the mines started to dry up. By the 1920s, Grandad Emrys' family was facing serious financial hardship, they had holes in their shoes, and they had to attend soup kitchens to survive. Fortunately, social reform was well underway and on 25 December 1927, the entire

Meek family was uprooted from Wales. They were taken to London where they spent a short time in the care of the authorities before being relocated to Luton under the nation's Poor Law Act.

The Grandad Emrys I knew was a funny old man who loved larking around with kids. He told tall tales and sang mad little ditties, like the one about some kid called John who'd gone to bed in his trousers on, and they sounded just as great in my grandad's lilting Welsh accent.

'Come 'ere, buggerlugs,' he'd say as I clambered onto his knee to listen to one of his yarns.

He'd often say things in Welsh and even spoke a bit of German which he'd learned during the war. Many of his tales were from the war when he'd been a gunner in the Royal Artillery. Oddly, the old man's nicotined fingertips were sort of rounded at the ends like lollipops. My dad said it had to do with his lung disease but Grandad's explanation was much better. He told me he'd been on lookout duty during the war and was peering over the edge of a trench when a tank drove by, running over and flattening the ends of his fingers.

I pestered him with the sorts of questions that all young boys ask: 'What was it like in the war, Grandad? Have you ever fired a machine gun, Grandad? Have you killed anyone, Grandad?'

He said he had but didn't confess to killing anyone, although I knew he'd seen some things that he wished he hadn't.

'Will you tell us one of your stories from the war,' I begged.

'Can't.'

'Why not?'

'I've got a bone in my leg.'

'What?'

'I'll tell you one about a bear, though,' he said, showing his bright white dentures and holding up his lollipop fingers like pruned claws. 'Grrrrrrr.'

He had a way of being able to turn something serious into something ridiculous and he liked to tell tales. On one occasion, as he slipped a Benson & Hedges from the gold packet and poked it in between his jelly lips, he told me the story of how the Meek family name originated from The Forest of Dean, a picturesque part of England which is close to the Welsh border. Grandad's eyes shone as he spoke of a family legend that had been passed down through the generations. It wasn't a long story but Grandad stretched it out between deep drags of his cigarette as he described the dark wooded villages and the poor people who inhabited them. 'They were all mostly coal miners and woodcutters,' he said. 'And they had to walk long hours through the mud to get to where they worked.'

Grandad Emrys explained how, long ago, one of those villagers, a member of the Meek family, had been among those responsible for killing the last wild bear that lived in the forest. He seemed proud to tell me this. 'And the Meek shall inherit the earth,' the old man sang, leaning back in his chair and extinguishing his spent cig in the glass ashtray as if to form a full stop.

I can't remember all the details of Grandad's bear anecdote and, of course, I never questioned any of his tales, but a quick rummage around Google revealed that the story was linked to a fairly well-documented incident which happened in the village of Ruardean in 1889. This was exactly one hundred years before Grandad's death and around the same time that the infamous Jack the Ripper was terrorizing the streets of East London. The bizarre legend has it that four Frenchmen were passing through Ruardean with their travelling show. They had with them two performing bears which they paraded in the local village squares in return for donations. Upon leaving the village, a rumour circulated that the bears had attacked a woman and a child. There had been a popular myth doing the rounds about foreign bear keepers feeding their animals on the flesh of children. This and the stories about the bears attacking anyone turned out to be complete fabrications but they proved enough for a mob of drunken men to pursue the Frenchmen, brutally beat them up, and kill the bears. One of the men involved in the incident was apparently my ancestor: a local collier named Thomas Meek, who was twenty-one at the time. The men were charged for various offences, with Thomas Meek being fined five pounds and sentenced to one month in prison for assault. This unfortunate incident became entrenched in folklore and disgraced the people of the village, the phrase 'Who killed the bears?' persisting for many decades as an insult. Even today, if you mention the tale of the bears inside any of the local pubs at Ruardean, you might get a frosty reception.

This documented story differs distinctly from the fabled affair which was passed down in our family. The somewhat skewed narrative relayed to me by my grandfather was that our courageous predecessor was, in fact, the local hero who saved the people from a vicious wild beast that ruled the forest. A sobering reminder of the blurred lines between rumour and reality and how people will often skim over or hide the dark and murky past.

Grandad's wife, Grandma Joan, was a strong-willed woman with a shock of stiff dark grey hair. She had a network of deep wrinkles on her baggy cheek wattles which I studied in the same way I'd studied the fissures and canyons on the leathery old maps at school. She was a lifelong smoker, as were all the adults in my world, and I would often wince from all the fag smoke as she chuffed away like a steam engine. A visitor to Grandma and Grandad's house would be forgiven for thinking that they had painted the entire inside walls and ceilings of their house mustard yellow, but they were just stained that colour by the nicotine which permeated constantly through the air. Fagnolia, my dad called it. And Grandma would gobble on those burning sticks while talking with the other adults. Just like all the others, she'd perfected the knack of being able to talk with the tab still hanging in the corner of her mouth and it would dance up and down as she nattered. The old woman could easily recite the latest gossip and chug down a whole cigarette without ever removing it from her lips.

With so many people around me always puffing away, I desperately wanted to know what the appeal was. So, making my way up to Grandma in her chair one day, I begged, 'Grandma, please let me have a go of your cigarette. Go on, pleeeeeeeze!'

She gave in and gently touched the damp freckled filter to my lips. I took the tiniest sip of smoke and the taste of a thousand dirty ashtrays filled my mouth. *WHOOSH!* It was as though I'd been injected with a toxic venom which instantly coursed through my insides and into my brain, making me go green and giddy. I ran upstairs to the bathroom, retching all the way, then held my tongue under the tap for ages, hoping it would wash the evil taste away. I decided there and then that I wasn't a fan of the ashtray flavour fag breath, or the nausea and lightheaded feeling that came with smoking. I never touched another cigarette after that.

Grandma also loved recounting her childhood stories as a young girl playing on cobbled streets in Nottingham and, one year, my dad drove us all up there in his father's blue Vauxhall Nova. It wasn't like my dad's van: it was clean inside and the headlights worked. The rain was slashing through the sky as we travelled north on the M1 but the windows were down to let the smoke out, so bits of sideways rain were gobbing in through the gaps. I was squished in the back with my half-brother Riki, Grandma, and Grandad. The traffic was stop-start and we'd barely made it past Toddington services when the first bad thing of the day happened. I was watching the water walloping down on the windscreen and then being batted side to side by the wipers. The steady hypnotic hum of the engine had me dozing off when I suddenly noticed the crimson splodge in front of us getting bigger and bigger. The engine's hum turned into a loud *sssshhhhhh!* And then there was a crunch of plastic as my dad pumped the brakes and we slid down the glassy road and ploughed into the back of a red Rover.

That was the only time I ever heard my grandad curse: 'Bastard!' he shouted as we made impact.

I was surprised and slightly amused by Grandad swearing. It didn't really count because his Welsh accent made it sound soft, almost friendly. Anyway, it turned out he wasn't even yelling about the crash. We didn't fly forward when the two cars collided because we were so tightly wedged in, like cigarettes in a pack. But Grandma gasped and as she threw her arms up in a panic, her tightly balled-up fist arced over my head and swung back down, smashing Grandad clean between the eyes. Grandad seemed to be quite annoyed since his glasses were broken and a bead of blood was dribbling down the bridge of his nose. My dad had already got out of the car and I could see the red Rover man getting out, too. My dad protested that it wasn't his fault because there was oil on the road. To be fair to him, I did see some rainbow patterns in the puddles and the windows *were* all steamed up.

Fortunately, we weren't going all that fast. So, apart from Grandad getting thumped, no one was hurt and, after some awkward pacing around by the adults and lots of pointing at the crumpled bumpers, we buckled up again and continued our journey to Nottingham.

We spent the afternoon wandering around the famous Goose Fair, where I took in all the strange sights and smells. They had traditional rides, as well as tents containing old-fashioned sideshows like Mouse-town and George the Gentle Giant. The adults ate mushy peas with mint sauce and I got some Mexican jumping beans.

In the evening, we went to a family event at some posh hotel. It was probably a perfectly ordinary hotel but it seemed posh to me. There was this fancy entrance with a buffet table where you could go up and get as much food as you wanted. Grandma and Grandad were off talking to their relatives and my dad was in the loo building a magic fag. Me and Riki had to keep a lookout, so we stayed outside, shunting up and down between the lobby and the buffet table—like a sort of sausage roll relay race, where we'd snatch an item from the table and dash back. I'd been told to be polite and say hello to all the distant relatives and extended family, including two girls who had come all the way from Canada. I had never met a kid from Clacton, let alone Canada, and I wanted to know more. *What's Canada like? Is it safe there? Are they kind to kids?*

I think the girls were like my second cousins or something. They weren't much older than me but I could tell that they were way smarter and more mature. They were clean and well-presented, with green ribbons in their thick glossy hair. I'd seen them standing in the lobby, watching us with their arms folded, and when I arrived back with my food, the older one strode over toward me. Even though she had braces on her teeth, I still thought she was still strangely pretty. She wore this beautiful raspberry red coat and had a beret perched at an angle on her head. My eyes lingered over the felt hat, which was red, the same as the coat, and it had a funny little stalk on the top, looking like a sprouting vegetable.

Everything about the girl fascinated me. She seemed different to anyone who lived on our estate and I imagined what it would be like to fly on an aeroplane to a place where kids are clean and confident and don't live in fear of being killed. I considered for a moment that maybe she wanted to join in our game and I tried to think of something cool to say but, by the way she was standing, I sensed that her approach was probably more business than pleasure.

'Hey, Car-l,' she said in an accent that made her sound like a robot. 'How ol-d are you?' The girl unfolded her arms and placed them confidently on her hips. I was surprised she knew my name; I didn't know hers.

'Er, ten,' I said, my mouth all stuffed full of cake.

Then, she looked me square in the eyes and hit me with it: 'Well, then, you should know be-dder, Car-l.'

Ouch! Her sister was standing behind her, hands on hips, as well, and I got this sudden urge to inspect the shiny marble flooring.

'You know this is a h-otel l-obby and not a playground, right? Right?'

I nodded at the veiny floor.

'Now, are you going to tell Ri-ki or should I?'

'I'll tell him,' I said, blowing out crumbs and trying to mash the cake back into my hot cheeks.

With that, the girl turned on her heel, and her glossy hair whipped around to follow her. I was dumbstruck. I'd just received a serious scalding from a schoolgirl; way worse than any thrashing from a grown-up I could get. I felt ashamed of myself and angry at Little Red Riding Beret for acting like an adult. It was the first time I'd ever been inside a hotel 'l-obby' and I didn't know the rules. Shortly after the ticking off, my dad came out of the bogs and said we were leaving.

***

Although Grandma could be argumentative, she also had a kindly and thoughtful side. The old dear kept a Littlewoods catalogue in her cupboard so I could leaf through the toys in the back. And she always saved me the little plastic gifts which were dug out from the dust in the bottom of her cereal boxes. Grandma Joan loved doing the crosswords in the paper and she'd always cut out any useful coupons. One year, she collected some vouchers which she sent off to exchange for tickets to Madame Tussauds.

Like many people of her generation, Grandma Joan never left the country. The only travelling she ever did was on the day trips to the seaside promenade at Mablethorpe. Her skin was olive coloured and my dad liked to tease her that the family derived from Romany Gypsies. But Grandma knew differently. Her maiden name was Carrier and she always said her family had French origins. She proudly told me about a famous ancestor of hers who had been in the French Revolution and she claimed that there was a picture of him in the famous London waxworks.

A couple of weeks later, the Madame Tussauds tickets arrived and we set off by train to London. Grandma was nervous about escalators, believing that the moving stairs would suck her under and mash her up, so I had to coax her on and hold on to her arm as we rolled down into the underground station. Once onboard the tube, Grandma got her spark back and she greeted strangers with her familiar 'Ey up, duck' as we travelled the three or four stops to Baker St. We walked along the busy streets and huddled amongst the tourists in the queue, silently soaking up the joy which coursed through the winter air. Grandma smoked a cigarette and adjusted the wooden buttons on her thick duffle coat one last time before we entered the impressive, green-domed building.

Once inside, we ambled around the maze, looking up at life-size sculptures of Ronald Reagan and Rick Astley. It was weird being up close to the stiff, glass-eyed celebrities staring out into space. The bit I liked best was a section called the Chamber of Horrors. It was a grisly gallery with gruesome models of notorious murderers and criminals from history. We wandered past wicked pirates and executed queens, keeping an eye out for any reference to the name Carrier. I was interested in all things grisly and macabre, so I paid special attention while scanning the exhibits and was first to spot him. Well, his severed head at least...

'Look, look!' I said to Grandma, pointing at the guillotined noggin of Monsieur Jean Baptiste Carrier. It was impaled on a spike with shiny lines of vampire blood dripping from the neck. We stood opened-mouthed, our eyes dancing as we studied the wooden plaque titled 'Carrier the Cruel'.

'Ooh er, looks like our ancestor was a bit of a rascal,' Grandma trilled as she read aloud from the wooden sign: 'French revolutionist who was sentenced to death by guillotine in 1794. Jean Baptiste Carrier, who was convicted of war crimes for pillaging the town of Nantes, murdering, and drowning 4,000 people in what was known as The National Bathtub.'

The plaque explained how old Jean Baptiste owned a boat and how he charged to ferry people to England, away from the French Revolution. Only the boat had a false bottom, so Carrier used to dump his human cargo out a few miles offshore and then go back for another load. At the end of the revolution, he was arrested, tried, and executed.

As me and Grandma stared at the head, it crossed my mind that now there were *two* tales of dodgy characters in our family history book, and both involved the ill-treatment of Frenchmen. *Must be something in our genes,* I thought as I waited to board the giant mechanical teacup which formed the final part of the attraction. And as we whizzed back around and out towards the gift shop, I wondered what else might be in our genes. Was I destined for more fear and death and confusion? Or was it possible that somehow, someday there could be a way out?

Chapter 12
Meek by Name

Wife: What were you like when you were at school?'

Me: A prat.

Towards the end of the school holidays, a week or so before I was due to start at Juniors, I was plodding down Strangers Way when a group of three or four gypsy boys spotted me. They were kids from the Irish travelling community whose caravans would often appear overnight. They set up camp in the park, sometimes accompanied by a couple of horses, and they'd stay for a few weeks or months before moving on, leaving behind piles of rubbish on the grass. Occasionally, the gypsy kids attended our local school but they mostly just roamed around causing havoc. They usually never bothered me when I was with my mates but now they had me on my own, they started roughing me up and rifling through my pockets. But I had nothing. One of them was a little lad with carrot-coloured hair flapping about his freckled face. He mainly stood behind the others, excitedly giggling and calling out, 'Git a hold of 'im, Kelly. He-he-he-he, check in his pockets, Kelly.'

He was talking to the stocky kid who'd been doing most of the rifling and seemed to be the leader. Kelly was lightly tanned, or he might've just been grubby, and he had a flattish nose with a scar leading onto his top lip. He wore a pink shirt which was neatly tucked into his jeans.

I knew it probably wouldn't do me much good but couldn't resist the opportunity to pipe up: 'Kelly's a girl's name. And pink's a girl's colour.'

I don't think the Kelly kid liked me saying that because, straight away, he cocked his head back and he gobbed right in my face. *SPLAT!* I could smell the slimy spitball sliding down my cheek. But I didn't stop to wipe it off. My instincts just took over and I lunged forward in an involuntary convulsion, slapping him in the mouth with a flurry of flailing windmill punches. *WHISH-DOOF! WHISH-DOOF!* Kelly must've been into American wrestling because he turned around and did that arm-pumping thing that Hulk Hogan did when he was mad. I continued the pummelling on his back until I got tired. That's when Kelly spun around and launched himself at me, punching me in the belly. *Wham!* That made me double over. And then he grabbed hold of me and we both fell on the floor. We drunkenly tussled on the tarmac, gouging at each other's eyes and ears, and as I yanked at his collar, I saw the layers of crusted filth around the back of the gypsy boy's neck. A few more manic headbutts, elbows, and twisted donkey kicks followed, and then our legs got entwined. He had a hold of my tired arms so I couldn't move and I struggled there, bucking and twisting, for some time. The carrot-haired pipsqueak was saying, 'Ahh, you've got I'm now Kelly, he's dead meat, he is.'

I could feel my shins and elbows grating against the gravel path. I didn't know what to do, so I yelled like I'd seen the American wrestlers doing on the telly: 'Yaaaaaaah!' Yaaaaaaah!'

The pipsqueak shouted, 'He-he-he-he! He's having a baby!' and the rest of them started laughing at me.

But they must have got bored of watching us grappling on the pavement because, after a few minutes of not much happening, they pulled us apart.

I wondered whether these traveller lads even knew anything about fighting. The first rule is that you never back down from a fight. And it's *always* one-on-one; you're not meant to pile in and help a mate out, even if he's getting whooped. I looked across at the Kelly kid, who was tucking his now-stretched pink shirt back into his jeans and smoothing down his curly black hair.

'We're gonna be at yer school next week,' he went, rubbing his hands together.

The carrot head, who I'd heard them calling Neil or Nail or something, was standing behind him and was getting all worked up and snorting like a little ginger jackal. 'Yeah, an' we're gonna git yer,' he brayed in his slightly Irish accent.

I felt sick for the next few days thinking about what might happen when I started at Leagrave Junior School. Of course, I was always a bit nervous about starting a new school. Will I make new friends? What will the teachers be like? But the only question on my mind this time was, were those gypsy boys going to make my life a misery?

By some miracle, those traveller lads never did come to my school. But I went on to have many more physical altercations: playground scuffles, street fights, muggings. Sometimes, I was the aggressor; sometimes, I had to defend myself from attack. I became hyper-vigilant, assessing the threat in anything that moved, while simultaneously trying to act like I wasn't afraid. I needed to be tough, like how I remembered Little Daryl had been. But being tough didn't help him much, did it?! Then again, he was only seven; and I was ten now. But I knew I wasn't tough at all; I was weak. But at least I had a way to disguise it: by walking with my shoulders back and my head up, accompanied by my best screwface. I hoped that acting hard would help to ward off the dangers that lurked all around.

I settled into Juniors school okay. I was liked and I had friends but I still had that uneasy itch that made me feel like I should be somewhere else. Leon was my *best* friend. He was strong and handsome, with tightly cropped Action Man hair and a caramel complexion. Still, he was the sort of slimeball who'd put on a cherubic smile whenever adults were around but, if there were no grown-us watching, he'd think nothing of booting a dog or lobbing stones at the ducklings by the river. He wasn't the sharpest knife in the drawer but he was good at sports and popular with girls and we'd play together every day. I wasn't as cool or as strong as Leon was but I think he liked me because he thought I was funny. We were in the same class and we'd frequently compete: who could spit the furthest or piss the highest. He pushed me over once when we were walking home from school and I fell backwards onto the stony path. As I reached out to break my fall, I slammed my hand onto a shard of brown bottle glass. The cut was deep and bloody, so I tried to imagine that I was holding a big blob of strawberry jam as I ran home crying.

The teachers never lasted very long at our school. Hired teachers always went off sick or left, making way for inexperienced supply teachers who couldn't control us. We used to run rings around them. We regularly had this lank-haired scouser bloke called Mr Smith who wore thick glasses and had bristly sideburns which dusted dandruff down onto his shoulders. Smithy was a jolly prick who always seemed to be trying to impress us with his lame stories, like how he never owned a TV or how he'd once lived next door to Paul McCartney. He never taught any actual lessons. Instead, he would ask us to copy from a book while he sat in his crumpled clothes, drinking coffee with a queer smile on his face.

During these periods, we did pretty much as we wanted. Some kids threw paper planes around. On one occasion, when the teacher left the classroom, I got up from my desk and wrote the words 'Smithy wanks' on the blackboard.

I'm not sure I even knew what wanking was at that point. But I did find out. It was one soggy grey morning in the third year. We were kept inside the classroom at break because of the rain and Keith Nash had crawled under one of the desks at the back of the room to do something nasty. At first, I assumed Keith was smoking because he used to bring bits of cigarettes into school sometimes and try to blow smoke rings in a corner of the playground. But this time, he wasn't smoking. Instead, he'd pulled his trousers down and was furiously hammering his hungry cock with a hard fist. He asked me to keep a lookout. That was wanking.

When I wasn't writing highly witty lines on the blackboard, I loved doodling and I'd use my time in lessons to create cartoon strips in the style of *Viz* and *Garbage Pail Kids*. My creations were inspired by mildly offensive characters such as Buster Gonad and Johnny One Note. And I used to staple the pages together to make comic books, which I sold to a boy called Jit for twenty-five pence.

Jit was the only Indian kid in the class. And the only kid who wore his hair in a side parting and had a strip of velvety bumfluff on his upper lip which formed the nascent notion of a moustache. He carried his books and pencils around in a briefcase. And on the last day of term, when we were allowed to wear non-uniform, Jit came to school dressed in his dad's military uniform. It was khaki and had gold buttons and bright embroidered emblems on it. He paid a heavy price for wearing that Indian army clobber as we sang Status Quo's version of 'In the Army Now' and subjected him to our casual racist taunts: highly creative insults which always revolved around saying 'Jit the shit' or 'Bud-Bud Ding-Ding'. What does that even mean? Jit took it in good stride, though, and he offered a few wisecracks in return. His dad ran a shop in Bury Park and Jit helped out there on the weekends. The kid was bright, industrious, and always smiling, even though his front teeth stuck out like a couple of Fox's Glacier Mints. He used to get these bags of sugary Indian sweets from his dad's shop and bring them to school to flog to the kids in the playground for a massive markup. Also, Jit resold my comic books for fifty pence a piece. This was my first lesson on how to hustle and turn a profit.

When there were no supply teachers available, the headmaster, Mr Forrester, taught our classes. He was a piece of work. A severe-looking man who always wore a grey suit jacket and a striped tie with a little badge on it. His half-moon spectacles hung around his neck on a chain. He was slight in build and had a wrinkly, freckly slaphead that looked like a ball bag. Mr Forrester put the 'old' into 'old school'. A professional educator, he was the kind of mighty dinosaur who commanded fear and respect and called all the boys by their surnames. 'Meek by name but not by nature,' he'd bellow when passing me in the hallway.

Forrester had been teaching for decades and had grown to despise children. His interests were cricket and disciplining children, and the regular teachers knew that if you misbehaved, all they had to do was to send you to sit on the naughty seat outside Forrester's office.

Mr Forrester once attempted to teach us about body image. He did so by hauling a girl called Karen Cook up onto the stage during assembly. The headmaster then pointed at various parts of her anatomy, her lumps and bumps, explaining to the whole school that the girl was what he labelled as 'heavy-boned'.

Another afternoon, when Mr Forrester had his back to us while he was frantically carving words onto the blackboard in his swirly, joined-up writing. We rested our heads on our hands, hypnotized by the rhythmic *tappity-tap-screech-scratch-tap-tip-tap* of the chalk against the wooden board. But the stupor was broken by the sound of a chair scraping at the back of the class.

'Drat!' Forrester yelled with his powerful tenor voice while slamming the piece of chalk down on the desk. 'Double drat!'

He quickly turned around and homed in on a kid named Steven Babbington who was snorting and fidgeting because he'd got a bit of rubber stuck up his nose. It was one of those small erasers from the end of a pencil and he was struggling to get it out. He'd got himself quite worked up in the process and was all red in the face.

The headteacher made Steven stand at the front of the class while he assisted in holding the boy's head and dislodging the nasal obstruction. 'Keep still… Stand up straight, boy!'

The piece of stationery was successfully dislodged from Steven's nostril, but now the boy was coughing and crying with increased agitation.

'Drat it all!'

We all looked on in silence as Forrester proceeded to ask the class if anyone had a spare training shoe in their gym bag. A kid named Paul Bambwo fired his arm into the air before the teacher had even finished his sentence, then sped out to the cloakroom. Paul returned moments later, holding one of those black canvas plimsolls that we used for PE. The headmaster took the gym shoe in his right hand and instructed Steven to bend over. The entire class gazed on agog as Mr Forrester whacked poor old Steven Babbington across the ass with the slipper. We twitched in our seats with every *BAFFF! BAFFF! BAFFF!* He must've spanked the boy a dozen times. *BAFFF! BAFFF!* We all peered down at our scratched desks when the defeated boy slinked silently back to his seat. Forrester then turned back around, picked up the chalk, and went straight back to his *tip-tappy-scritch-tap* again like nothing had happened.

***

During the weekends and on school holidays, Mum did her best to work and keep order, to inform and inspire us while maintaining a clean and tidy home. But being a single parent with three chavvy sprogs knocking around must have been exhausting. She'd always be saying funny things like 'yous are doing me head in' or other variations like 'getting on me wick' or 'grinding me patience'. And my favourite: 'I'm fed up to the back teeth with yous.'

Leon's mum was probably the same because she used to turf him out of the house first thing, so he'd come straight over and knock for me early on those fresh bright mornings.

Knock-knock. 'Lossie, comin' out?'

He'd wait outside in the street while I got ready and then we'd go and call for other boys. We prowled the neighbourhood, looking for things to do. Even though we knew Jit wasn't allowed to play out with us, we called occasionally anyway. His mum would offer tins of Coke and packets of Monster Munch on the doorstep. I don't know why she did this. Maybe it was customary Indian hospitality, or maybe she just took pity on us. Either way, we didn't care. Free food's free food.

Me and Leon roamed the streets, smashing up discarded TVs and hi-fis, setting off fireworks, and making prank calls from phone boxes. We raced up the stinky staircases to the top of the flats where, from the landing, we could see rows of pylons stretching out for miles across the fields like giant metal scarecrows. We had an aerial view of the motorway snaking its way north and south and we'd spit down at the tiny ant-like figures crawling on the streets below us. We vaulted over fences and shimmied up drainpipes, onto sheds and porches. Signs that read 'DANGER' and 'KEEP OUT' were tempting invitations to us: a green light to explore building sites and investigate burnt-out vehicles which were still smouldering from the previous night's inferno. Sometimes, we followed the dried-up riverbeds and crept through the dark, slimy tunnels which linked up with the river that flowed beneath various roads. I was squelching my way through one of those underground passages near Leon's house once when a rusty nail went through the sole of my shoe and buried itself in my foot. Leon's mum took me to A&E where they gave me a tetanus shot.

Most of our attempts to quell the boredom involved petty vandalism and things like kicking balls against peoples' walls until they came out shouting: 'Sod off! Go on, scram! The lot of you!'

As soon as the livid neighbours went back in, we'd start up again.

Occasionally, we'd look for a stronger hit to quench our appetite for excitement and so seek out the more unhinged characters in our community. Local oddballs and fruitcakes who had nicknames like Dogend Daisy, Bananaman, and the notorious Red Devil. We often waited by the local shops for a man called John the Junkie. That wasn't his real name but it's what everyone called him. John the Junkie always had a pocket full of Kit Kats and he'd dish them out to us on the condition that we returned the foil wrappers so he could save them for 'his mate Mr Brown and his pet dragon'. *What a total nut job!*

We used to taunt these neighbourhood crackpots from a safe distance, shouting abuse at them until they gave chase. Then we'd run like the clappers across the park, giggling as we went. Getting a chase was a real thrill. Much better than the rides at the fair.

Often, we would hide out in the safe haven that was the school, crouching down behind the wall, wheezing like asthmatics, our sides hurting from all the laughing and running. On weekends, we could easily hop over the school wall and be free to roam the no-man's land of the empty playgrounds at our leisure. I enjoyed practising the long jump in the sandpit behind the field. And I was getting quite good at it, 'til I realized that the sand was full of cat shit. The school was a series of squat, single-storey brick boxes which looked more like huts or bunkers than a school. We'd give each other bunk-ups onto the low roofs so we could scour around for any balls which had been booted up there during term time.

One summer afternoon, me and Leon were messing around on those flat shingle roofs with a couple of other boys including this hard kid called Neil McGonigle, who always wore a plaster cast on his left arm. If he ever really had a broken arm, I don't know, but I think he just used it to get out of PE lessons and hide things, like the long pointy screwdriver he kept wedged inside there. The other boys were on the other side of the roof, kicking gravel at each other, and I was lying on my back, watching the cumulus and stratus clouds and the seagulls squawking overhead like a gang of rowdy skinheads. *Keee! Keee! Keee!*

Stupid seagulls! Why's there's always stupid seagulls scrapping 'round the school, anyway, when we're nowhere near the sea? They can't be 'ere for the food.

I was using the corner of one of the skylight windows as a pillow and, when I turned my head to the side, I realized it was loose. I hauled myself up and called the others over to investigate. Neil McGonigle slid his screwdriver out from his plaster cast and undid the couple of loose screws that remained on one side of the window. Then we hooked our fingers underneath the rubber seals and tugged at the flimsy plastic dome. It lifted away softly like a door of a spaceship. We all peered down into the vacant school and smiled at our discovery. A pirate's treasure trove.

We did a quick scan around, then descended onto a bookcase and carefully lowered ourselves into the silent room. We had landed in an annexe: a musty old storeroom of some kind, used to house instruments, science equipment, and costumes for the school plays. It was strange to be inside the school when there was no one else there—no kids making a racket and no teachers to tell us off. We crept around for a while in the strange stillness, flinging piles of paper onto the floor and snatching up fistfuls of colourful counters and paperclips to stuff into our pockets. But Neil McGonigle got overexcited and kicked over the bookcase which crashed to the ground, setting off an alarm. It was loud and the sound echoed along the empty hallways.

'LEG IT!'

Bits of bright shrapnel dusted the ground as we gathered up our souvenirs, repositioned the bookcase, and emerged back outside. From up on the roof, we spotted a police car turning in through the school gates, so we draped down the side of the building and scarpered towards Deadman's Alley. That was the name given to the shallow wooded embankment which ran parallel to the M1 motorway. I don't know why it was called Deadman's Alley. If a dead man was ever found along that strip of wasteland, I never heard about it.

The motorway traffic was rushing back and forth a few metres away as we frantically scaled the wire fence. We entered the narrow passage which was littered with sooty trash and broken vehicle parts and, as we clambered our way through the brambles, I took a final glance over my shoulder and saw the police car reach the playground just as we slipped out of sight.

A fortnight later, we were back at school, sitting on our bony asses in assembly after just having murdered a rendition of 'All Things Bright and Beautiful'.

'The school was subject to a break-in during the holidays, and we know who was responsible,' Mr Forrester said, scanning the rows of children with his sneaky eyes. 'Items were stolen and a list of names has been handed over to the police.'

I had my head bent over so as not to give myself away, and I was holding onto my ankles to try to steady my quaking knees. My heart was racing. I was certain I was going to end up in the children's home for my crime. But a few uneasy days went by, and then weeks, and it eventually became evident that old scrotum head was bluffing. We had got away with it. He'd had no idea who did the break-in and it was never mentioned again. Neither by the teachers, nor by us.

March 2020

Growing up, I definitely had my share of 'why me?' moments where I felt hard done by and wished that I had a father who got up before midday and wore a suit to work (or even a pair of overalls for that matter). Moments when I likened myself to Charlie Bucket from *Willy Wonka and the Chocolate Factory*. My mum still calls me Charlie, and whenever I was down as a kid, she used to sing a song from the 1971 musical starring Gene Wilder: 'Cheer up, Charlie, just be glad you're you.'

Not that I was often miserable (I was saving that for later); I was a mostly contented child. On the occasions I have spoken to people about my childhood experiences, I have been met with tight smiles, doughy eyes, or awkward silences. Perhaps people just don't know how to respond. Or maybe they feel an element of guilt that they were better off than me. But we're all fragile and damaged in some way. We're all walking wounded, carrying our baggage and scars of our pasts. Sure, I wasn't born on a bed of roses, but I never believed I was deprived. I didn't know any different. I'm not saying that my boyhood was a breeze but I'm learning that the past does not define or dictate my world, and I'm beginning to understand how I can create a new, better one going forward.

Besides, I wasn't the most unfortunate kid in my school. Not by a long stretch. Plenty of others suffered far worse afflictions than me: children who were well known to social services and who probably went to bed cold and hungry and without anyone tucking them in. Children such as the timid twig-like girl who lived on our street. Let's call her Sally. One morning, when Sally was nine, she discovered her alcoholic mother dead on the couch. She was given some time off school to recover and when the girl returned two weeks later, her school uniform was all creased and she smelled like wet dog. Sally was made to sit out of assembly while the whole school was told about how she had developed alopecia due to the stress of the tragic incident. We were asked to be kind and supportive towards Sally because she had suffered a horrible trauma. And I watched as, immediately after the assembly, a group of scuzzy boys ran up to her, pointing and barking, 'Baldilocks and the Three Hairs.'

Another girl in my class was a chunky mixed-race girl who, for the purposes of this story, we'll call Charmaine. Her mother was never home, so Charmaine was left to fend for herself and her two picky-headed brothers. This meant that Charmaine was streetwise and us boys knew not to mess with her. Charmaine was also an aspiring arsonist and, one day, when we were in the third year, she smuggled a lighter into school and set fire to her own hair. I was standing in the playground when I saw the cloud of smoke come billowing from the girls' cloakroom. We were all herded back inside and we watched out of the classroom window as an ambulance raced through the main gates. A week later, Charmaine returned to school with a new hairstyle and a scabby forehead.

Another example I'll throw in for good measure was the school nitwit, a boy we called Nutty Nigel. He used to eat Tip-Ex and spent most of his break times hiding in the dingy computer room. Nigel came from a decent family, outside of the estate, but he never stood a chance at school. When he was eighteen, Nigel strangled a local pensioner with his dressing gown cord. I read in the paper that my former classmate kept the corpse in a cupboard for a month and decorated it with fairy lights while pilfering the old codger's Post Office account.

And then there was the boy I'd known as Little Daryl. Whom I'd heard had been stabbed or poisoned or both. The boy I'd been too afraid to ask about. Anyway, no one seems to know about him anymore. He's been rubbed out like a wrong answer. As though no one cares. Except me. Maybe people would rather forget. Because it was such a long time ago. And anyway, like my mum said, a lot of stuff went on on that estate.

Chapter 13
Sink or Swim

Fatty and Skinny were in the bed. Fatty blew off and Skinny was dead.

Playground rhyme

Martin was outside with his shirt off. He was working on his rusty old Volkswagen campervan which he'd bought for five hundred pounds off his mate who had the unfortunate name of Terry Bater. The van was mostly blue, though it was dotted with rusty scabs and bogey-coloured patches. Martin loved that van but I thought it looked like something out of *Wacky Races*. He spent hours polishing all the shiny metal bits and fiddling with the engine that was hidden under a flap at the back like a little gurgling belly. If the weather was nice, he'd pop up the stripy roof and let us play inside.

If Colette from next door, who was always steaming drunk and twitching her net curtains, caught sight of the colourful vehicle, she'd come flying out waving a fiver in her slippers and hair curlers. 'E'ya'are, love, gi' us twe'ty Embassy and a box of matches, will ya, love?' It would take Martin some time to convince her that he wasn't the ice-cream man.

Martin had bought the camper so he could run a stall at the market selling Pepe Jeans. Me and Sophie would be woken up at 4 a.m. on a Sunday and we'd get carried out in our pyjamas and bundled into the back of the van with all the piles of stock. I think the market must've been in London because it took a long time to get there and, by the time we did, it was light. We knew when we were there because we'd be jerked into life by this booming voice going, 'Jumbo, Jumbo, it's the big one!'

The first time I heard it, I thought it might be something cool, like a singer or a children's entertainer, but it was just a beardy man selling hot dogs. And it was annoying because he kept on shouting the same thing over and over, all day long.

Once our stall was set up, I was given a bacon bap from the beardy man and allowed to go off and play with the market kids. They were rough and they knew how to hustle. I'd follow them as they weaved around the different stalls asking for empty plastic bags. You could buy all sorts of things at the market. It was a bit like a car boot sale but much bigger and the prices were written on giant yellow stars. And it didn't matter where you were—you could never get away from the booming voice and the sweaty onion smell which wafted from the beardy man's trailer: 'Jumbo, Jumbo, it's the big one!'

The market kids said we needed the strong plastic bags for what we were gonna do, not the flimsy ones. And once we'd collected enough, our little gang headed over to the furthest end of the market and climbed over a hill and into a claggy field, where a man was operating a strange contraption. The man pulled a lever on his machine and it fired little black frisbees up into the air. More men were standing at the edge of the field, trying to shoot the frisbees with guns. I learned from the market kids that these frisbees were called clay pigeons. Once the men stopped shooting, we were allowed to go into the field and pick up all the unbroken ones. And if we returned with a full bag, we'd be given fifty pence.

Our days at the market were spent squelching around in the field, searching for intact clay pigeons. There was no sense of danger as we rummaged in the field like pigs looking for truffles. And it didn't take us long to fill a bag. We'd squelch over to the man with the machine and collect our fifty pence, which we then used to buy shitty plastic toys off one of the stalls. The only danger I encountered was when I ended up falling into a deep muddy puddle. I was covered head to toe in brown goop and Martin made me spend the rest of the day inside the camper. Sitting on the threadbare seats in my pyjamas, I had to spend torturous hours watching the market kids playing with their toys through the steamed-up windows while listening to the beardy man on repeat: 'Jumbo, Jumbo, it's the big one!'

We went on loads of trips in Martin's blue hippy mobile. The inside of it leaked and it stank of stagnant piss but I didn't mind because travelling in it was an exciting adventure. We could go to places that weren't Luton. Like Milton Keynes or the museum where they had stuffed animals and a little wooden box with fleas in it, and if you looked through the microscope, you could see the fleas were wearing clothes. Mad!

The camper was good because we could fit more people in the back and Martin would let Leon tag along sometimes. Like the time we went to some country park and me and Leon stuck our fingers up at the other kids as the van bucked away down the street. It was a hot day as we rattled along in the old biscuit tin. The radio was at full volume and we took turns to stick our heads out of the window so our faces flapped in the wind. Martin liked to go really fast down the hills, so the engine went *putt-putt-putt* like one of those old-fashioned warplanes. Meanwhile, we'd be bouncing around in the rear, experiencing that happy-sick feeling you get from the belly rides at the fair.

At the country park, while the adults lazed on a blanket under a big tree, me and Leon would steamroll our way through the long, dry grass. I loved exploring the woodland and rolling fields which hummed with life, lapping up the sweet summer air and looking under logs for earwigs and Charlie pigs. On the edge of the grass, there were these sandstone mounds where I was surprised to see these small, speckled lizards. Some were lying perfectly still like they were sunbathing, and others were busily darting about amongst the moss and purple heather. I was a bit hot and sweaty from all the running around, so I went and sat with the adults. I was taking a long swig of warm orange squash when I remembered how Martin had told me he'd caught lizards when he was working in the Middle East.

'Oi, Martin,' I said, 'there's some lizards over there. You know how to catch lizards, don't ya?'

He nodded, puffing out his chest a little. 'Yeah.'

'Pleeeeeeeze, Martin, will you get me one? Pleeeeeeeze?'

Martin scrambled to his feet and I showed him the place where I'd spotted the lizards. He must have been telling the truth about the Middle East because he was a master lizard catcher and easily snapped one up for me. It was brown and green and about as long as my forearm. I asked Martin to let me bring it home and he said I could, so I carried it in the back of the van, gently cupped in my hands. It took all the patience I had not to sneak a peek.

When we arrived home, I parted my hands by the front-room window to take a glimpse at the shiny reptile. As soon as it saw light, the thing zipped across the window ledge with a flash of its golden tail. I panicked and did a judo-chop motion with my hand to block its path. But I misjudged it and whacked the poor creature straight across its back, killing it instantly. I was devastated. Another innocent life was unduly extinguished.

I turned the slender corpse over a couple of times in my hand. Its eyes were still open but its scales had lost their gleam. It reminded me of that episode of *Grange Hill* where a kid called Danny Kendall was found lying dead in the back of a car. Scared the shit out of me, that did: the way the boy was all dull and pale and just staring out into space. It got me thinking again about how a kid could suddenly just get killed and stop being alive. I laid the dead lizard out on the window ledge for a while to see if it would come back to life but it didn't, so I chucked the limp carcass into the dustbin. And Leon called me a murderer.

Time went by quickly at Juniors and, in the second year, the whole class got rounded up and bussed down the road to the Lewsey swimming baths. This happened every Tuesday morning and the aim of the trips was to teach us to swim. All the boys were sent into a dirty room with long wooden benches where we danced about on the slippery floor and thrashed each other with the sharp corners of our towels. The echoing changing room had cracked tiles and rusty pipes, and the caustic toilet smell bit into your nasal passages. After we'd changed, we were led in single file down a narrow corridor and forced to navigate a recessed pit of cold vinegary water which had scummy plasters floating in it. I think the purpose of the festering footbath was to stop the spread of things like foot fungus and verrucas, but we did our best to skip over it.

We were placed into groups according to our swimming ability. Some kids were natural water babies and already knew how to swim. Some even had accessories, like swimming caps, goggles, rubber socks, and nose clips. I was put in the section of losers who waded up and down the shallow end, flailing their thin arms and legs.

It was on a weekend shortly after I had started the school swimming lessons that Martin decided to take us for another trip in his van. Leon was allowed to come again. Adults in the front, kids in the back. I don't know if it was because I'd been going on about my swimming lessons but we drove out to one of those huge indoor water parks where they had a slide and a wave machine.

Leon went straight at it, diving and frolicking in the waves with some other boys, but I still couldn't swim, so I just waded in up to my knees. I stood in the shallow end by myself, watching the boys from a distance as they came shooting out the end of the slide before they'd urgently climb out of the pool and go racing back towards the ladder. Some other children were playing on inflatables and a mum was gently splashing with her toddler. When I looked down at the rippling water, it seemed to be luring me in, daring me to test out what I'd learned during the swimming lessons. Curiosity got the better of me and I decided to edge in a bit deeper. I guided my feet down the gentle slope and when I realized that I was on my tiptoes, I tried to go back. But the force of the wave machine tugged me out until I was clumsily treading water. By now, the water was up to my chin and no amount of thrashing was dragging me back to where I was. I found myself flailing as the water reached my mouth and I started taking in large gulps. I could hear the waves slapping around my ears and all the other noises just blended together like the roar of a crowd at a football match. I slipped deeper and deeper until I was all elongated like one of those rubbery Stretch Armstrong toys that I'd always wanted. Soon, my nose and eyes were the only things bobbing above the water and all I could see was the top of the slide. Now, everything was quiet apart from the underwater *glug-glug* and the sound of my heart thumping. It felt as if I were being buried by quicksand or spiralling down a plughole. I carried on churning away with my arms and legs but I was exhausted.

Suddenly, there was a rush of cool air. I opened my eyes to see I was enveloped in the thick arms of a burly man with a bristly face and a hairy torso. He was carrying me out of the water. I was all floppy but some energy crept back into my muscles as the man set me down by the side of the pool. I was back amongst the echoing din of the swimming baths now, which I added to with my retching and gasping. The whole place was spinning, my teeth were chattering, and I felt sick. I rubbed my stinging eyes and just about managed to whimper a thank you to the hairy man as he walked away. My legs were still trembling but I pulled myself up and staggered off to find my so-called family.

As I teetered by the edge of the pool, I saw a big sign that read 'POOL RULES'. Underneath, it said, 'NO RUNNING, NO SHOUTING, NO BOMBING, and NO PETTING.' And right at the bottom, it said, 'PARENTS SHOULDN'T LET CHILDREN SWIM ALONE.' The bombing sounded like fun and I didn't know what they meant by petting, but the rules were written in big red letters which meant they were important. I read the last one again: 'PARENTS SHOULDN'T LET CHILDREN SWIM ALONE.' But if it was so important, why were they letting *me* swim alone? Wasn't *I* important? As I looked around, it seemed like a long time had passed and I wondered where I'd been. But I knew I hadn't been anywhere because everything was still exactly the same. I could see the kids on the inflatables and Leon and the others were still sploshing in the waves and clambering back out towards the slide. I'd thought I was being tough by venturing out into the water, but no-one had even cared. I was nearly drowning but they all just carried on as normal. It made me think about my old friend Little Daryl and I wondered what he would have thought about me trying to be tough. But he couldn't have thought anything because he was dead. And no-one had cared about that, either; they'd just carried on as normal.

As the year went on, I continued to plug away at the school swimming lessons, splashing around for the next two years, determined to improve until I eventually passed my red ribbon by jumping in and completing a width of the pool. I went on to get my blue by picking up a brick from the bottom and treading water for thirty seconds. In the third year, I even earned my green ribbon by demonstrating backstroke in my paisley pyjamas.

The coloured ribbons and certificates were given out in assembly. I proudly displayed my ribbons which my mum sewed onto my trunks for me. I've never been what you would call a strong swimmer but perseverance and a desire to say yes to life saw me through. Perhaps hearing about what had happened to Little Daryl gave me the urgency to make the most of my life. I really don't know. But whatever the case, I was sure I'd have died that day if that vigilant stranger with the hairy torso hadn't hauled me out of the pool.

***

It wasn't long after the swimming incident that I discovered the joys of permanent marker pens and, one Friday, I smuggled one into school. I don't know where I got it from but it was likely stolen as I can't imagine my mum had any reason to keep a marker pen in the house. During lunchtime, I decided to unleash my creativity by doing a bit of street art in the school playground. I took the pen out of my pocket and doodled my special signature motif onto one of the wooden benches: a cock and balls. I took my time, adding a veiny shaft and a line of something squirting out of the helmet. I stood back and admired my artwork. But just like the circumcised willy on the bench, my design career was to be cut short.

It turned out that the weasel-faced caretaker had been spying on me from the window in his little room and he'd gone and snitched on me to the headmaster. When I returned to class, I was immediately summoned to Mr Forrester's office. I sat outside, anxiously fidgeting for a full twenty minutes before he eventually ushered me into the familiar room with its ribbed grey carpet and varnished wood panelling on the wall. I was made to stand in front of his desk, which felt as big as a Starship Enterprise. It was a shiny, oval-shaped desk with a notebook and some sharpened pencils lined up on one side. I looked at the shelves on the left-hand wall, neatly stacked with thick books and cricket stuff. Mr Forrester was sitting bolt upright on the other side of his desk. He always sat bolt upright. He had his hands clasped together on the surface of the desk and I could see the furrows on his freckled forehead as he squinted over the top of his glasses.

'Meek but not very mild,' he said.

It turned out he'd already had the school secretary, Mrs Taber, call my mum to inform her of my serious misconduct. *This could be bad.*

Mr Forrester appeared to read my mind and seemed excited. He was interlocking his knuckles and wiggling back in his chair. He pushed his glasses back towards his face. 'Do you know what your mother thinks of you, boy?'

I wanted to answer with something clever and cheeky like, 'Yeah, and everybody thinks *you're* a big old ball-bag-headed bastard.' But I didn't. I just clammed up and kept staring out the window.

'She thinks butter wouldn't melt in your mouth,' the headmaster chided before explaining to me that defacing school property amounted to criminal damage and that he intended to press charges. 'The police are en route to the school at this very moment,' Mr Forrester uttered with a slight smirk forming in the corner of his mouth.

I had no idea what Old Ball-Bag-Head was on about. Why would I try melting butter in my mouth? He said a bunch of other stupid stuff, too, about crimes and justice and strong arms of the law. But it just sounded like a load of old nonsense, like when grown-ups spoke on the *Snoopy* cartoons. 'Wap, wap, wa-ha, wap, wah, wah, wah.'

Then Forrester sent me back to class where I had to spend the rest of the school day awaiting my fate. This time, I was certain that the Old Bill were going to burst into the classroom, handcuff me, and cart me off to juvenile prison.

But the police never showed, and neither did Mum, so it wasn't until I got home that I had to face the music. My mum was already there when I got home from school, as usual, doing the washing up. She turned around and looked at me thoughtfully as she told me how Mrs Taber had rung her up that afternoon and told her that I was in trouble with the police. I raised my eyebrows and tried to feign mild surprise. She explained that, not knowing what to do, she had called my dad. I'd no idea what she'd said to him but I knew that it must have taken some desperation for Zoe to ask my father for help. He was usually too strung out to be of any assistance.

I'd go on to flirt with petty crime and have minor brushes with the police as an adolescent but, as a young kid, I only really smelled a whiff of them. Like the time when me and Leon were mucking about, hanging on the iron railings of the steep slope that was up the top. Cars were sweeping past below us and, when we got to the traffic lights at the end of the bridge, a bulgy-eyed bloke folded his tattooed arms across his broad chest and accused us of bunging stones off the bridge and breaking his van's windscreen. We hadn't. Not intentionally, anyway. The man took our names and addresses and said he was going to pass them on to the police. Leon had the sense (or the balls) to give bogus details. I feared that the Old Bill would come and pay us a visit, so when I got home, I thought it best to come clean. I put on a solemn face and gingerly explained to my mum what had happened. She closed her eyes and said she was disappointed. I don't know whether my mum knew it but hearing her say that was somehow worse than getting hit or shouted at. The lack of anger and agitation had a way of sending a cold vibration through my bones, really making me think I'd done something truly wrong. My mum wasn't dumb, so perhaps that was her intention all along: to rattle and guilt me into behaving. Or perhaps she was genuinely saddened that her solitary efforts to steer me away from trouble were failing. Maybe she was concerned for my safety and worried about what sort of trouble may be yet to come.

But on the occasion the secretary called to complain about my graffiti, my mum didn't say she was angry or disappointed or anything like that. Neither did she say any more about my dad, so I supposed he hadn't given any useful advice in the end. She just rolled the saggy lids down over her big eyes and slowly exhaled, like a balloon that was having all the air let out of it. Then she turned around and carried on with the washing up.

The next day, I didn't see Mr Forrester or hear anything else about the trouble I'd been in. And after school, Leon called for me and said that his mum had invited me over for dinner. While we were at his house, slurping on tinned spaghetti hoops, Leon's mum put her hands under her chin and looked at me from across the table. 'So, what happened at school this week?'

I knew what she was getting at and that there was no point in lying. Leon's mum was a dinner lady and she knew everything that went on.

I shrugged. 'Dunno. Got done for drawing on one of the benches.'

'What would you say to Mr Forrester if you could tell him anything?' Leon's mum asked.

Leon took advantage of this rare opportunity to swear in front of an adult and responded instantly and confidently: 'I'd call him a shit-bit.'

We giggled, and then they both looked at me. I bowed my head and stayed silent.

'Go on,' Leon's mum said, 'you can whisper it to me if you like.'

I got up and circled the table, then serenaded Leon's mum with the worst profanities my ten-year-old brain could muster. She looked at Leon and pulled a face like she was embarrassed by my raw critique of the sadistic schoolmaster. But after I sat down again, she told me how she'd heard that my dad had been down to the school and pinned Mr Forrester up against his wood-panelled wall in front of Mrs Taber.

Huh? I was surprised...and I felt a strange warmth and pride to know Dad had done me one of the few fatherly services of my life. A bit unconventional but credit where credit's due.

When I saw my dad on the weekend, I told him what I'd heard and asked him if it was true. But he didn't give me a straight answer. He just shot me a crooked grin and said, 'Sounds a cock and ball story to me.'

The following week at school, I noticed that my illustrations had magically disappeared from the bench. And I never again found myself sitting outside the office of The Grand High Ball-Bag-Head.

March 2020

I usually avoid watching the news because I find it all a bit depressing. But I'm visiting one of those huge American warehouse stores that have all the high-end electrical items piled up at the entrance and, as I weave past the audio-visual section, there's something on one of the display screens that piques my interest. I stop and stare at the seventy-two-inch plasma. They're talking about a virus outbreak in China that's supposedly spreading to other countries and everyone's overreacting, going out and buying loads of toilet paper. Sounds odd. I stretch my neck and scan around the store towards the exit. It's true! I can see it for myself. It's 10 a.m. and people are leaving the store with trollies piled high with nothing but loo roll. I turn back to the TV screen open-mouthed. There's a government minister on there saying that they might have to shut down all the schools and public places and all that. But I can't see it happening. It's madness. Perhaps in China but not here. I carry on with my shopping and, as I steer my trolley through the busy warehouse, I wonder why I'm feeling so heavy and unsettled. Can't be this stuff about the virus: it's just a storm in a teacup.

Maybe it's because I still haven't followed up on what happened to Little Daryl. I'm not exactly sure why I haven't. Perhaps subconsciously I'd rather *not* know how he died. I feel like I owe it to my little friend to write down all the facts of his death, if I can only fucking find them! But what if knowing the truth only makes things worse? Or what if I learn something hideous about myself at the same time?

A week later, I'm having lunch in a Luton chicken shop with my wife and our two kids. By coincidence, Leon walks in with his son. Leon has retained his youthful good looks but he's got his hair braided and is covered in tattoos. The conversation quickly turns to the times we shared when we were younger, including reminiscing about the sleepovers we used to have at Leon's house. I couldn't have friends to stay at mine as I shared a bedroom with a toddler. But Leon had his own room. The box room, it was called, and it was more box than room because it sat directly above the stairs.

'Do you remember how we'd climb up and jump down onto the single bed?'

Leon's eyes light up. 'Yeah, I used to practise my wrestling moves on there!'

My wife and kids are listening quietly as we talk quickly and scoop up greasy bits of chicken with our fingers. I mention my Barry McGuigan boxing gloves and how we used them to wallop each other in the face.

'We used to knock lumps out of each other, din't we? Doing the Ali shuffle and wildly swinging hooks to the head and body.'

I confess to Leon that my jaw still creaks from those encounters.

'Perhaps *that's* why we called it the box room,' Leon says with a smirk, wiggling his jaw from side to side. 'Look, mine's the same.'

'Oi, what about the time when we both played the ugly sisters in the school play?' I say, and Leon's face splits into an ear-to-ear grin.

In the first year of Juniors, it was announced that we were going to perform *Cinderella* for the annual concert. Heidi Metcalfe took the role of Cinderella and a popular black boy named Dexter played the prince. While the teacher was deciding on who to cast for the remaining roles, someone put their hand up and suggested that two boys should play the ugly sisters. Everyone laughed because the idea seemed so far-fetched but the teacher paused and thought about it for a moment, then she smiled and called me and Leon up to the front of the class.

On the night of the performance, Leon and I entered from the back of the hall, surprising the audience with our wigs and make-up. We pranced up and down the stage in our dresses and high heels like seasoned pantomime dames. The audience roared with laughter as we flicked our hair and recited our witty one-liners with perfect comic timing. I'm not a natural extrovert but I felt comfortable being on stage and I'd go on to have more leading roles in school plays.

I think that my early exposure to a variety of people probably helped to make me a confident communicator. Or what my siblings might describe as a jumped-up, ingratiating tosspot. Perhaps being around lots of strangers when I was younger instilled in me a necessity to show off and jostle for the spotlight, my instinct for self-preservation urging me not to become the shrinking violet that my surname connotes. Either way, I certainly realized quite early on that if I was going to stand any chance of being heard and getting what I wanted, then I needed to speak up.

That must also be why, when I played the ugly sister, I did as I was told. I stood up straight, focused on the brightly lit exit sign on the back wall, and I projected my lines loudly and clearly. The creative process and the results that could be achieved by making stuff pleased me. If I had been born in a place where these things were seen as actual jobs, I might have fancied my chances of becoming a comic or an actor or an artist or a writer. I guess, secretly, I *did* feel that I was a little bit different from my peers. Like I knew something that they didn't. Like I had special access to another place, removed from fear and disappointment, where I was more than I was. I've been called a snob in the past and accused of having ideas above my station but I believe it was these formative experiences which equipped me with the courage to try out new things. And the feeling of possibility has stayed with me throughout my life.

'That was funny, that was,' I say to Leon. 'Wonder if anyone's got it on video.'

I get up to leave the chicken shop and Leon starts wiping off the grease off his heavily inked hands. He offers me a limp handshake and I show him the jagged scar which still sits across my pale palm. I tell him it's from the time he pushed me over in the park but he says he doesn't remember. In fairness, I might have forgotten about it, too, if it wasn't for the meaty badge etched into my flesh. As I turn my ageing hand over to examine the scar for myself, I notice that the squiggly silvery line is flaking around the edges. It looks like a question mark and the tissue around it is peeling off in a way that I haven't seen before.

'It was good to catch up and talk about the old times,' I say to Leon as I put on my coat.

He looks me in the eye and nods, and I realize that us talking about the past doesn't do it justice. Somehow, the words aren't enough. It was only in those short moments of stillness, in between the words, that we both knew where we'd been and what we'd done.

Chapter 14
A Lead!

I remember Luton
as I'm swallowing my crout'n.

John Hegley

Apart from its airport, the only other famous thing about Luton is the football team. Luton Town Football Club was founded in the 1880s but the team had their most successful period in the 1980s. They first tasted glory under manager David Pleat in 1982 when they won the league and were promoted to the first division. Then, in 1988, Ray Harford took over as manager and they beat Arsenal to win the cup at Wembley Stadium. They were 2-1 down in the last ten minutes but managed to save a penalty and score two goals. It was a time of riotous joy in the town. Luton Town fever took over and all the shopfronts and pub windows were draped with orange flags and bunting.

Like all the other kids at school, I had a Panini album for collecting and displaying football stickers. We'd flip through our little stacks of cards at break time saying, 'Got, got, need, got, need, need.' Liverpool was top of the league at the time, so we knew all the players' names: Peter Beardsley, John Barnes, Ian Rush. Luton Town's headband-wearing captain, Steve Foster, even came to our school once to give a talk; a few of the boys got his autograph in their sticker albums but I was off sick that day.

I liked playing football. I'd been taught to dribble the ball up and down the street by the bigger boys, so I was quick and I had patience and judgement. And so, I was alright at it and deemed good enough to join the school team. For our first away match, I was chosen to play as the centre forward. It was an unpopular decision among my teammates as Leon was always up front, while I usually played along the wings. The match was against Ferrars Juniors. They looked smarter and more organized than us and seeing them come out in their kits with their dads cheering them on gave me that squelchy feeling in my tummy. I think the pressure of being the centre forward must've got to me because I just started blindly bombing up and down the sloped pitch, punting the ball in all directions. At one point, I got confused and dribbled the ball the wrong way. Then the muddy ball came flying towards me, smacked off my knobbly leg, and went straight into our net. Own goal! I felt like a right idiot. It made sense to me to stay alert and to look where I was going but with all the adults shouting aggressively from the sidelines, I just couldn't keep focused. The only good bit was when we were given slices of orange at half-time. We ended up losing the match 5-0.

The next game was at home against another local rival, Pirton Hill. I was told I was going to start on the bench as a substitute.

My so-called teammates booed and made fun of me. They said that my new position was right back: 'Right back in the changing room.' Then they all started singing 'Su-ub, su-ub' which was short for substitute but, in my mind, meant sub-standard. Naturally, I started having that horrible feeling again that my mates—the ones who were meant to be looking out for me—weren't really on my side. I sizzled with rage and decided, there and then, that I wasn't going to show up for the match. I just picked up my kit from the cloakroom and strode home.

To this day, I've never played football again and I can't comprehend why many men get so emotional about the game. Why they pledge lifelong allegiance to a particular team and then allow the success or failure of said team to dictate how they feel is beyond me.

Unfortunately, my unwillingness to follow the sport meant I'd often struggle to answer that inevitable question which is always employed to break the ice between unknown males: What team d'you support?

I once made the mistake of responding to a friend's dad with, 'Hmm, I'm not really into football.'

My admission seemed to anger him, and he replied with, 'Well, what are ya, then, some kind of gaylord?'

I went as red as a beetroot.

After that, I decided that the best option was to compromise my integrity and attempt to feign an interest in heterosexual sports: 'Oh, yeah,' I'd say, followed by, 'I support...[insert popular team name here].' I'd use that line hoping that would be the end of the conversation but it was rarely the case. They would usually follow up with another question or comment about a particular player. Leaving me exposed as a football fraud. Or worse: some kind of gaylord.

Maybe that was part of the reason I was beginning to feel less and less at home in my hometown. As everyone around me was attaching their passions and dreams to football, I was slowly waking up to the idea that maybe there were other ways to live, in new and different places.

My short football career wasn't helped by the fact that my dad wasn't the kick-a-ball-in-the-park sort of dad. Emrys never attended any events or sports days. In fact, my dad had zero interest in sports, except boxing. He'd grown up under the reign of Ali (then Cassius Clay) and his father had taken him to Luton Boys' Club when he was a youth where he had learned to box and competed in several amateur bouts. But Emrys lost interest when he discovered weed and women.

As a well-known smoker, my dad developed a wide circle of friends who respected him as someone in the know when it came to matters of marijuana. Most of his druggy mates lived in my area, so he'd usually take the opportunity to visit them after picking me up. By the time I was nine, eating fish sandwiches at my grandparents' was a thing of the past and my dad's pick-up times got later and later. I'd sit up on a Friday night, watching TV with my mum until there was a knock at the door. Then I'd spend the rest of the evening driving around with Emrys as he dropped off packages, collected cash, and hung out with his 'bredrens', blazing bud while nodding their heads to dub-reggae beats by the likes of Sister Carol and Linton Kwesi Johnson.

But my dad didn't lose his love for boxing entirely and on one of those evenings while I was with him, Mr Beresford invited us over to his place to watch a big event: Mike Tyson vs Frank Bruno. Mr Beresford was a retired Jamaican man who used to work with my dad at the hospital and they'd bonded over their mutual love of marijuana. He lived in the flats next to my house. I never liked going into the flats, where the separate lifts for odd and even numbers confused me and sharp sounds and smells bounced through the long narrow passages. The only thing I *did* like about those buildings was that they had cable TV.

'How comes everyone in the flats gets to watch Sky and we've only got four channels?' I asked my dad as we arrived that cold February evening.

'The council's put free cable in all the flats to keep everyone indoors. So they don't have to deal with all the social problems,' my dad replied.

'Huh?' I didn't know anything about social problems. All that mattered to me was if I could get Sky TV so I could watch American wrestling.

I could've watched the rubbish English wrestlers, like big Old Daddy and fat Giant Haystacks, on normal telly but they weren't very good. Instead, I took any opportunity I could to catch a glimpse of Hulk

Hogan and Macho Man Randy Savage, even if it meant going into those stinky flats. My dad took the piss out of the WWF wrestlers, saying that they were morons. He said American wrestling was fake, while boxing was real. But it didn't matter what he said because I knew the American wrestlers were way better than the English ones: those shouting meatheads were the idols of all the boys at school.

We stepped into the dimly lit fetid capsule which transported the residents up and down those skyward-pointing structures. The stainless-steel interior of the lift was *stained* with dark sticky fluids and the grotty floor was covered in layers of flattened fag butts and years of packed-down grime.

'Da-ad,' I said, poking my head into the deep recess on the back wall of the elevator, 'why do they have that big gap in the back of the lift?'

'That's where they stick the coffin when someone pops their clogs,' my dad responded matter-of-factly. I stepped away from the recess and looked up at him in disbelief. 'Wha's the matter son?' he said shrugging 'A dead person can't stand up in here, can they?'

'Huh?'

'They'd go all floppy, wouldn't they? Well, unless they'd got rigor mortis, I s'pose.'

I remembered that he'd said something similar when I'd asked about the giant chimney stack at the hospital: 'That's the incinerator where they burn all the bodies and bits what get chopped off.'

The doors juddered shut and we held our breaths under the flickering fluorescent light as we ascended to the twelfth floor. As we exited the lift, my dad must have seen me turning to take another peek at the hole in the wall. 'The dead won't hurt ya, son,' he said with a chuckle. 'It's the live ones you wanna be worrying about.'

We filed along the corridor, and my dad rapped his knuckles on the second from the last door. The tiny flat smelled of gravy and there were pictures of cute Rastafarian children on the walls. Mr Beresford waved us inside and told me that I could call him Uncle Beres. I liked the old man because he knew how to make banana fritters and he told me stories about all the street fights he'd had in his younger days. He opened the fridge and pulled out a tray covered in tin foil, then he crouched down beside me to show me what we were having for dinner.

'Look in a de ting, bwoy', Mr Beresford said, eagerly peeling back the foil and pointing at the few seasoned bits of stringy meat which lined the tray. 'Mek hair grow 'pan your chest.' He smiled through his grey beard and made some strange hand gestures. 'Cow cod soup.'

I thought that maybe it contained meat and fish, which sounded weird but bearable. We ate the soup with banana, which was also weird, and while it tasted okay, it was a bit spicy and a bit rubbery. I politely chewed through my bowl of soup and, afterwards, my dad told me that we had been eating a bull's penis. I was outraged.

Later that evening, when the wrestling was on, I started practising my body slams and I spewed all over Mr Beresford's settee. I don't know if it was because of the excitement of being allowed to stay up late or some kind of dirty protest about the schlong soup. My dad saw me yack but didn't do anything but take another puff on his joint and carry on talking. Nothing could derail Emrys when he was in mid-conversation, or high, or both.

Shortly after that, I crashed on the settee. Someone must've cleaned up the barf, though, because by the time I was awoken for the boxing, it was gone. My dad and Mr Beresford were perched on the edges of their chairs, shouting at the telly. I struggled to keep my eyes open throughout, though I did manage to see the end. Mr Beresford and my dad were on their feet now and Mike Tyson was charging in and biffing Frank Bruno in his head and body. *(Biff, biff.)* And poor old Frank's head jolted and his knees buckled. *(Biff.)* And then the referee man jumped in front of him and waved his hands in the air to say the fight was over.

And as I got older, I realized that my dad was correct in his assessment of those American wrestlers as morons. In fact, I started to realize that I share several traits with my father—probably more than I'd like to admit. My reluctance to watch or participate in any sports, except for boxing, for one. But perhaps another similarity is my desire to see the world differently than those around me. When everyone told Emrys what to do, he did the opposite. When everyone made me feel like I was meant to stay in Luton, I started plotting my escape.

May 2020

This coronavirus thing escalated quickly and brought the whole world to a standstill. I didn't think it would have this much of an impact but it's the biggest world event that's happened in my lifetime and has caused major disruption to pretty much everything. At first, it was just an interesting interruption, an impromptu diversion from our daily lives. Almost fun.

But the novelty has worn off now and it's starting to get everyone down. The kids are off school and pretty much all my work has dried up. I'm feeling miserable and my routines have gone out of the window. The aching dullness of the day means that my mind becomes a hive of activity at night time.

I'm lying in bed and it's well into the dark hours. My wife's asleep next to me. I'd like to be asleep, too, but my bastard brain won't let me. It keeps inventing pointless scenarios, like what I'd do with a million quid or how I could run away and make myself disappear—that sort of thing.

When I do eventually drift off, I dream that I'm in some dingy room or apartment somewhere. There's a gloomy yellow half-light coming through the window and while I'm lying on a single bed, I can hear the grizzly sounds of a murder happening in the adjacent room. The walls are paper thin and there's all this groaning and clunking and screaming. It's the middle of the night and I realize that I know who's being murdered. It's a guy. I know him. His name is Daryl. Somehow, the murderer is aware that I am listening and now he is trying to get in through my door. I manage to escape from the building and soon find myself outside my childhood home, standing between the parked cars in the street.

I wake up with a racing heart and a dry throat.

Over the next few days, my thoughts keep returning to Little Daryl. I make a note of the dream in my diary and I ruminate on the sadness and frustration of not being able to glean any information about what happened to him.

Suddenly, an idea slides into my head. I retrieve a forgotten memory. Like an email or a letter. A message in a bottle I've been waiting for.

It's weird how some memories are filed away. Yet others are forever bright and vivid as if they had only just happened. Then there are those that are like lost pharaoh tombs, waiting to be exhumed after years of being buried.

This particular memory is patchy and unfocused but it feels legit. I'm with my mum at Luton cemetery. I must have been eight or nine years old. My mum laid some flowers on the grave of her grandparents and I started looking at the nearby memorials. (In the same way that I liked visiting hospitals, I've always felt at ease in graveyards. To me, they've always been peaceful places.) Somehow, I ended up at the far side of the cemetery in the children's section. The memory is *very* faint now but I recall seeing Little Daryl's grave. It had his name and picture on it. The same picture they had shown on the TV. The one of him in his knitted jumper and helmet hair.

I've read in the self-help books that our unconscious brains shift and warp our dreams and memories over time. Is this a false memory? But it feels real. I definitely recall seeing a grave and knowing it was him. I snatch the idea from the air and store it away before it disappears again for good.

A few weeks later, after the government eases the lockdown rules and permits non-essential shopping, I find myself driving over to my native town of Luton. During my adult life, I have elected to domicile in various parts of the planet. But in the last few years, I've returned to reside in a place which is only ten miles from where I grew up. I once read a study somewhere which claimed that more than half of people live within fifteen miles of their childhood home. Many never leave, but of those that do move away, the majority return by the time they are middle-aged. I suppose this could be for economic or practical reasons, like being close to friends and family, but I wonder whether it may also be for reasons closer related to comfort, emotional security, and familiarity. I guess I will always be from Luton and, even though I'm not particularly fond of the town I grew up in, I often feel that I'm intrinsically linked with it, like it forms a part of who I am. As if I was made by it.

I park up at the cemetery and navigate my way along the pathways which lead through neatly manicured gardens and past the lines of tombs separated by stout shrubs and hedges. It's a sunny day and I move briskly, instinctively knowing where to go. I sniff out the children's graves like a bloodhound. I know I'm in the right place but I find nothing. Negative thoughts invade my head. *Another dead-end,* I tell myself. The familiar doubts creep in. *Did it even happen? Did Daryl even exist? Have I invented the whole thing? Am I looking for a figment of my imagination?*

I start to become despondent but decide to give it one last shot, so I head over to the crematorium office. The wood-clad room is filled with the sharp, pissy smell of ageing flowers. A pudgy man is sitting behind the desk, looking like one of those little Buddha statues with his rounded shoulders and his egg-shaped head. He's wearing baggy jeans and a leather waistcoat.

'Excuse me, sir,' I say, 'I wonder if you can help me find a specific grave? It's of a child.'

The waistcoat looks up. 'What's da name?' he grunts in a cockney accent.

'Daryl,' I say. 'I think he died sometime between 1986 and 1988.'

Waistcoat pushes up off his seat and waddles out into the back room. I can see him leafing through some huge heavy books which I presume contain the names of hundreds of dead people. His shirt's hanging out the back of his waistcoat. After about a minute, he raises his head and calls out to me from the back room: '31st March 1987,'

I quickly swallow. 'Er, yeah.'

'Dat's da burial date,' he adds.

He comes back through and scribbles down some numbers on a yellow Post-it note. I feel itchy. He slides the yellow note across the desk. I snatch it up.

'Dat's section five, Kids. Row nine, grave fourteen.' He stabs one of his stubby fingers down on the scrap of paper.

'Thanks for your help,' I say and quickly head over towards section five.

I find it easily: it's right where I was looking before. I find the row and count along until I get to number fourteen...but he's not there. I walk up and down a couple of times and count from the other end, making sure I have the right spot. I count again. Nothing, I scratch my head, baffled.

I make another inspection of the yellow note and, as I look up, I notice that there's a gap between the graves thirteen and fifteen. I kneel in front of the empty space and realize that the headstone has been removed. I eagerly scrape at the earth with my fingers; there's definitely something buried beneath a couple of inches of sandy soil.

An older gentleman is silently tending to a grave just a few rows up, so I go over and ask if I can borrow his trowel. I scratch away at the cool damp soil but all I find is a broken stump of concrete and the faded shard remains of a porcelain puppy. It's a forgotten grave, like those ancient decaying monoliths you see covered in moss and ivy. But it's worse. The memorial stone has gone. It feels like someone has gone to the effort to erase this dead boy from existence. But why?

I console myself that at least I have some information. A name. A date. A lead.

The search continues.

Chapter 15
New Kids on the Block

Skinny malink melodeon legs umbrella feet,
Went to the pictures and couldn't get a seat.
When the picture started,
Skinny malink farted.
Skinny malink melodeon legs umbrella feet.

Irish children's song

Christmas of 1990 came around quickly and was the best one yet. I shuffled into the front room early that morning and I saw the pile of gleaming presents under the tree; Mum had saved hard and really gone to town. My eyes were drawn to something large propped against our rickety table. I went straight over to the item which was loosely wrapped in coloured paper and knew instantly what it was! A brand-new bike!

I was thrilled and could hardly believe my eyes. I wanted to jump up and down and shout, Woo-hoo! Fuck me! It's only a brand-new fuckin' bike! But I didn't. I played it cool. I *was* proper dazzled, though. I really hadn't expected that.

The cold I'd been complaining about during the days leading up to Christmas was soon forgotten as I excitedly tore off the remaining strips of thin tissue paper from the bike. Then I quickly got dressed and went out for a ride around the block.

I felt free, like the big man himself on his sleigh, flying around those empty frozen streets. Now, I had a way to transport myself to new and different places. The few people who were out and about stopped and smiled: they could see that I was enamoured with that beautiful red Raleigh Mustang.

As well as receiving the bike that year, I got all the usual stuff: colouring books, felt-tip pens, and a shit load of selection boxes. And there was this Michael Jackson videotape which I watched on repeat until I learned how to do the moonwalk. Auntie Tracy even gave us all a joint present: a Nintendo. I was made up. Although I no longer believed in Father Christmas (by then I was old enough to know how it worked), the wonder and magic abounded.

I pedalled that damn bicycle everywhere: to school, to friends' houses. I'd even volunteer to run errands just so I could go out and ride it. There was this one Saturday morning when my mum sent me to the Co-op to get a tub of Stork and a loaf of white Sunblest. Nothing out of the ordinary; I did it all the time, returning home with a carrier bag swinging from my handlebars. But this Saturday morning *did* turn out to be different because I came out of the shop to find my bike was gone. I knew it must have been nicked by one of the zombie crackheads who hung around the shops but there was no sign of them or the bike. I was gutted. That bike was my ticket to new and different places and I'd only had it for a few months. I trawled every nook and corner of the estate. For weeks, I looked in back gardens, bins, garages, and alleyways. My mum even got Fat Daisy to put out a few threats but the Raleigh was never returned.

But so what, who gives a shit anyway? Worse things had happened before and there was probably plenty more to come. I just needed to grow up. Suck it all up and take it like a man.

Looking back, I reckon the time my bike got stolen was probably when I started abandoning my embarrassing childish inhibitions and growing more self-conscious. My worldview was becoming tinted with a dark lens and I had decided that the world was full of dangerous people who were out to get me. Despite their flaws, my parents cared for me and did their best to provide a stable home life. But external factors and the environment around me were already shaping my core beliefs: society was untrustworthy and corrupt, and I was always going to be hurt and let down.

Of course, I wasn't aware of any of this yet, and it would be a long time before I'd even begin to understand its complexities. But the potent churning emotions behind it had already taken root within and they were starting to manifest in my attitudes and behaviours.

A few months later, we got a council exchange to a bigger house several streets away. A council exchange does what it says on the tin: two tenants do a straight swap of their council-provided residences. But like with any transaction (whether you're trading properties or football stickers), one person always ends up with the shitty end of the stick. That's what happened on the day we were due to move. Martin had just loaded up the campervan with all our stuff when he got wind that the geriatric couple who had agreed to swap houses with us had changed their minds. While we were out in the street, saying goodbye to all our friends and neighbours, my mum told an angry Martin, 'Leave it out, will ya?!' But Martin said he was just gonna give the old lady some gentle persuasion. So, he jived over there and started waggling his arms about and puffing out his chest. Whatever he said or did, the deal was back on, so I pulled on the dog's lead and turned to walk across the estate towards our new home.

I was ten and Sophie was seven when we moved into that house. She got the dank box room and I had to share with Little Tommy Fucker. The place was old and in need of decoration; I suppose you could say it was run-down. There were exposed floorboards in the living room and a few bits of second-hand furniture. And a balding brown carpet lined the stairs. I'd heard someone say that the houses on our street were made out of breeze blocks, left over from building the nearby flats. That sounded about right because our house was always breezy in the summer and cold as an ice block in winter. On those bitter mornings, the condensation on the insides of the windowpanes would freeze and we'd all huddle around the industrial-looking coal fire which dominated the front room.

Our new house sat within the long shadow of another different block of flats. This looming tower block was called Home Court, though it was anything but homely. I walked past those sinister taupe-coloured tenements every single day. Pigeons and carrier bags whizzed around them in the wind and you could find all sorts of weird stuff around the base of the flats, too, because the people inside couldn't be bothered to use the bins and just chucked their junk out of their windows. Once, I found a whole collection of dead goldfish.

And it was always blustery around there, as if the air which forced its way between the towers was constantly angry. For entertainment, I'd unzip my coat and lean into the great currents, stretching out my arms like Superman while my hood flapped behind me. Other times, I'd just stand at the end of our street and watch people doing silly walks through the wind tunnel as they returned home with their shopping. Occasionally, my patience was rewarded with the sight of someone getting caught by a gust and falling over.

Our estate was mostly populated by blacks and Irish which is a fact that I was oblivious to at the time. I had been around people of all shapes and colours from an early age and just assumed everywhere was like that. I thought my half-brother Riki's year-round tan was attributed to his eczema; it just didn't register to me that he was mixed race. Kids are in tune with real and important stuff like energy and emotions and toilet humour. There's an innocence and naivety—an indifference—when it comes to boring ideas made up by adults; concepts such as religion, class, ethnicity, and politics. Many of my school friends were black or 'half-caste' as we called them. Leon's skin had a warm honey hue while the rest of his family were white. It was never, ever questioned or even mentioned.

In the school playground, we told dirty jokes and traded insults. They nearly always included the word gay. But a particular favourite was to point at anything gross and say, 'That's your mum, that is.' And we made up silly acronyms like, 'Yo, are you a BMW? A Black Man's Willy?' And the reply would be something like, 'Naaah, man, you're an ABC. An African Bum Cleaner.' These quips weren't used in a hateful way; they were just meant to be rude and funny.

I first realized that the subject of skin colour was of importance to some people when I saw a group of black boys huddled together across the yard. They had formed a line, side by side, with their arms linked over each other's shoulders, and were gaily skipping around. This was nothing unusual as it was the method used by boys to get other boys (never girls) to form a gang and join a game. Sometimes, they chanted things like, 'Who wants to play foo-oot-ball?' But today's chorus was, 'Black is power, white is sour.' The words didn't mean anything to me.

I just wanted to be part of the cool kids' game, so I eagerly joined the end of the line.

The black boys were tough and they didn't take any shit because their parents had taught them to be proud and stand up for themselves. Their families had come to the UK years before and they had fought and struggled to be accepted in society. Their struggle was far from over but, by the 1980s, progress was being made and black music was gaining popularity. Many of our sporting heroes were black, too, and reggae-rap culture was making its way into the mainstream pop charts. The black 'youts' were 'runnin' tings' in our school. Words in Jamaican patois, like 'innit', 'battyboy', and 'rassclart' peppered our everyday vocabulary. We said 'arks' instead of 'ask'. It was cool to be black and hierarchies were formed depending on whether you could fight, rap, or run fast. Black kids could gain extra credits if they were of Caribbean rather than African descent, and a light-skin pickney might get a hard time if they had a black mum and a white dad.

The advantage of having black friends was that nobody messed with me. Words to the effect of 'Yo allow him, man, he hangs around with the Fosters, innit' saved me from altercations and meant I could mouth off as much as I liked.

The Fosters were a well-known Jamaican family who lived in Home Court. Every time I walked by the block, I heard the sweet reggae music wafting out of their open windows. That cramped bedroom was occupied by four roughneck brothers and Marlon told me that the radio was constantly playing music, even through the night.

Marlon was my friend and the youngest of the Foster brothers. His slicked-back hair formed a serpentine swoop on the top of his head and, like the rest of us, he had learned to walk around with a twisted screwface expression. Both his mum and dad lived at home but they seemed to let him do as he pleased, he possessed no toys or games like other kids our age, and he had been schooled in the ways of the streets by his older brothers—teenage boys who were bad news, and so everyone assumed Marlon was headed down the same crooked path.

But I knew he was a good kid at heart. I took pleasure in being friends with Marlon, not just because it brought me status but, also, because he showed me warmth and he was super smart. We were in the same class at school and we devised conniving tricks to befuddle the teachers and win floppy, dog-eared merit cards.

But while Marlon's quick ability to pull strings and curry favour impressed me, he liked to lash out for no reason, and that made me afraid of him. We could be sitting in the library or lining up for PE when I'd feel a heavy thump on my arm or the sting of a cuff upside my head. One time, I retaliated and slapped him across the face with a plastic ruler. I wanted to be closer to Marlon than I was but his short temper kept me at bay. I was worried and confused by his angry outbursts and began to view him as just another mean kid that I needed to keep a watchful eye on. I couldn't figure out why Marlon was so mean. Perhaps his violent tendencies came from experiencing things that were unfamiliar to me. Things like racial discrimination, uncaring parents, and fistfuls of tough love doled out by big brothers.

One Monday morning during the school holidays, Marlon and his brother Tyrone inducted me into the art of shoplifting. The three of us slid into the Co-op and headed straight down to the sweets aisle. Tyrone palmed a KP Choc Dip and handed it to me. I looked at the shiny blue plastic cup with its two separate sections, one for the chocolate and one for the finger biscuits. Tyrone grinned at me, flashing his gold tooth, and nodded towards Marlon's hood. I immediately understood the assignment. I dropped the cup gently into the hood, snatched up a pack of Chewits and some Refreshers, and we breezed out of the shop. I marvelled at how easy it was. We carried our spoils around to the back where I clumsily fished the stolen cup out of my friend's hood. Marlon already had his hand outstretched like a spade and I willingly delivered the goods. I watched on as he peeled back the foil lid and slowly scoffed down the entire confection.

The alley at the back of the shops was a good place to hang out. It was strewn with ripped bin bags that spewed out broken glass, syringes, condoms, shitty nappies, and all kinds of other things. It was a place for us to forage and we found useful stuff there sometimes, like out-of-date food or broken stereos. One time, we discovered a damp pile of mucky magazines, all neatly packed into a gym bag.

From our alley lair, we spied a girl we knew from school, Lindsey Gadd. We looked over at her with disgust as she stood like a scarecrow on the turd-covered scrub of grass next to the shops. The Gadds were a trampy family who lived on Barley Lane, the shortest and most run-down street in Luton, where most of the houses had broken windows and washing machines in the front yards. The Gadds were the kind of people who isolated themselves from the community and acted like everybody was watching them. They had gaunt faces and cold sores. They wore jack-up trousers and had hideous homemade haircuts. Everyone stayed away from the Gadds at school because they had nits. The teacher once asked the class if anyone had any pets and Lindsey Gadd raised her hand to say that she had some rats at home. She explained how the rats were mostly friendly but, sometimes, they bit her and her brothers while they slept.

Because Barley Lane was the road next to ours, Lindsey and her brothers often showed up while we were playing outside. My mum would make jam sandwiches for them and they'd just sit there and smile on our front grass like Cabbage Patch Kids dolls.

I fished out an empty Lucozade bottle from one of the bins. I took out my willy and wazzed into the bottle. Why not? But I could only fill it halfway, so I handed the bottle to Marlon who topped it up. He screwed on the lid and we went over to offer the bottle of piping hot piss to Lindsey Gadd.

'Alright, Lindsey,' I said. 'Bought this drink but I don't want it now. You can have it if you like.'

The scarecrow girl took off the lid, sniffed it, and then took the tiniest sip from the bottle. 'Oooor, it's wee!' Lindsey Gadd gurned as she poured the remaining contents onto the grass.

These pranks were no more than a fun distraction for us but, as I write down these memories now, I am filled with a foreboding sense of guilt and sorrow. I feel a burning heartache for the fact that I handled my own bad feelings by picking on children like the Gadds who already endured unthinkable suffering and neglect. Marlon, Tyrone, and me laughed until our knees buckled. We were totally oblivious to our savagery and I was unaware that I would carry the weight of shame with me for years to come. But at that moment, we didn't care. We felt alive. We were rude boys, ragamuffins, and thieves.

This all happened when I was nearly eleven and my mum had turned thirty. She'd started reading books in the evenings and eating grapefruit for breakfast and I wondered if it was because she wanted to try to steer our family ship towards calmer seas. Maybe Zoe saw moving to the new house as an opportunity to set anchor.

But Martin had other ideas. His own vessel continued to drift and rock in different directions and his drinking got worse.

I was used to stormy weather and being awakened at night. I'd lie there, fitfully listening to the arguments, the yelling, the banging. Sometimes, he'd leave for a few days. During that time, there was no more burnt toast and Martin's stuff started disappearing. Even his books of Green Shield stamps that were banded together in the back of the cabinet.

And then, late one night, at around midnight, I heard him shout the words, 'That's it, I'm fuckin' gone! For good!' The door slammed and Martin vanished.

And that *was* it. His ship had sailed.

Well, for several months, anyway. He showed up again on Christmas Day, lingering in the doorway like a grey cloud. But he didn't stay long. And we hardly saw him at all after that.

Occasionally, Sophie and Tommy got an unannounced visit when he'd turn up looking ill and dishevelled. He'd take them out to various squats and grotty places where they'd have to sit and watch him sip lager and do drugs with his mates. Sometimes, I tagged along with them, to a squalid house in Dunstable where Martin and his buddies eagerly showed off a giant blue pyramid they'd built out of empty Tennent's Lager cans. But we were less than impressed.

I wish I could say that I looked out for Sophie and Tommy during those difficult times—that I was a caring and protective older brother—but I didn't. I wasn't. I never showed the slightest semblance of sympathy or support for them. Instead, I held their toys out of reach and teased them. I gave them muscle pumps and snake bites and Chinese burns. And I dangled drools of dribble over their faces, which I'd suck back up at the last minute. I didn't wish my brother and sister harm exactly; I just looked out for myself. And I felt safer when Martin wasn't around.

***

It was 1991 and the Berlin Wall was down. Thatcher was gone, Mandela was free, and something was kicking off in Iraq, but I didn't give a shit about any of that. My primary concerns were: (A) what trainers I had, and (B) who was the toughest in school. Martin and his camper were long gone but Earl and Fat Daisy were still knocking around. One or the other would often show up drunk when they had nowhere else to go. They would loiter on our sofa for a day or two and I'd take advantage of their condition, pestering them for money 'til they tossed me a pound coin so I could go buy my *Smash Hits* magazines. Leafing through those glossy pages filled with pictures of pop stars and song lyrics made me happy.

One day, I went with Grandma Joan to the Arndale Market after school. I had a pair of LA Gear on my feet and I needed a shell suit to compliment my fresh tramlines. So, we ferreted around looking for one under the strip lights of the indoor market, past the joke shop and the heaps of dull-eyed fish and speckled plantains. I loved going to the indoor market because it offered me a glimpse of alien life which existed elsewhere: a cavern of tantalizing colours and exotic sounds and smells; a place where you could buy anything from a shalwar kameez to vacuum cleaner parts or a Vietnamese river cobbler. We wandered through the warrens of canopies until ten pounds was finally handed over and a tracksuit was stuffed into a thin plastic bag. The sports-jacket-and-trousers ensemble looked like a crinkly bin liner with red, yellow, and green stripes down the arms. It was classified as sportswear but it would have been completely useless in any kind of athletic scenario as even the slightest gust of wind would have caused it to puff up like an inflatable blimp.

I'd planned to wear the shell suit on my birthday. I was excited about turning eleven and had invited some boys to come over after school. I rarely had friends over because I was afraid of them seeing all the rocks of cannabis resin which were weighed into eighths and quarters on the brass scales. Or the ripped remains of Rizla packets which had been torn up to make roaches for the long Bob Marley cigarettes that my mum and her friends smoked.

It was a warm Friday afternoon in May as I hurried out of the school gates, whipping off my stripy tie and stuffing it into my pocket. I felt the sun on my face and the sweat pasting the shirt onto my back under my bag as I rushed home. I took a shortcut through a neighbour's garden by squeezing through a gap in their back fence. I couldn't hang around because they had a dog and, one time, it chased me and pinned me up against their garden shed. Once home, I bounded straight upstairs, removed the baggy suit from its bag, and threw it on. I went into my mum's room to look in the rectangular mirror, which was propped against the wall. I was satisfied by the image of a pre-pubescent Michelin Man standing before me. When Marlon Foster arrived, he looked my outfit up and down and sucked his teeth. 'Ya fuckin' eedyaat! You cyan't wear dem colours,' he said, referring to red, gold, and green colours of the Rastafarian flag which were emblazoned down the sides of my new clothing.

I was crushed and confused; I'd just wanted to look cool. The word 'wigger' hadn't yet been invented, and it would be another two decades before I'd learn the term 'cultural appropriation'.

A few weeks later, my mum accidentally melted a hole along one side of the acrylic tracksuit with the iron. I was secretly glad to lift the lid and stuff the shell suit into the dustbin as I hadn't planned on wearing it again.

Leon and Keith Nash came over that afternoon to celebrate my birthday, as well, and we all mucked around in the back garden, shooting each other with water pistols. I squirted Keith in the crotch and made a joke about how he'd wet the bed. It must've hit a nerve because Keith went batshit. He started lurching around the house and kicking furniture. Me and the other two boys watched on in amazement as he slammed the door before running upstairs and throwing himself on the floor of our tiny cubicle bathroom. As the man of the house, I couldn't just stand by and watch him wreck the joint, so I dragged Keith back down the stairs and out onto the scrappy lawn where I gave him a kicking. He didn't fight back and, afterwards, I felt bad about the whole thing. Maybe it was the shell suit jibe that had sparked my rage, perhaps I was still confused about things that had happened in the past, or maybe Keith was just a prime target for me to display my manliness. I don't know. Either way, we made up and celebrated my birthday with a ham and pineapple pizza and a bottle of Irn-Bru. Later, I blew out some candles which had been pressed into the top of a Viennetta ice-cream cake.

My dad showed up the following day with a bloke called Manny: a stringy suntanned guy who wore dark glasses and looked like a cockatoo. He had a crest of golden hair which was thin on top but long at the back. Manny and my dad had previously worked together at the hospital and they playfully recounted stories from their time there. I listened closely to their tales of wheeling stiffs out to the morgue and I giggled when my dad teased Manny about his role of prepping patients for theatre, which involved shaving off their pubic hair.

After moving on from his pube-pruning position, Manny had emigrated to Australia. He was back in the UK visiting friends and family and I took the opportunity to learn all about his adopted home. I was intoxicated by the notion of exotic places and pestered the guy with questions all day: 'How hot is Australia? How big are the spiders? Do you know Harold Bishop from *Neighbours*?'

Manny generously indulged me in my interrogations, answering my questions rapidly, with busy eyes and theatrical hand movements. He even showed me his boomerang (not a euphemism) and some photographs of unreal-looking rock formations. And then, he produced the coolest thing I had ever seen: a snakeskin which he carried around in a circular tin. My eyes widened as Manny unrolled the light-brown skin which had been dusted in talcum powder. He told me of how he had slain and skinned the animal himself with his bare hands. Just like a real-life *Crocodile Dundee.* From then on, I referred to Manny as 'The Snake Skinner'.

Emrys rarely looked after his appearance, usually choosing to throw on ripped jeans and a sloppy jumper with burn holes in it. But on this particular day, the spidery figure was draped in a pair of glaring Bermuda shorts and a candy-coloured surf shirt with the words 'G'day from W.A.' scrawled across the front of it. They were gifts which The Snake Skinner had brought him from Western Australia and it looked like the two of them were having a competition to see who could look the most ridiculous. Emrys had even had his hair cut and bleached and, on his feet, he was wearing black-and-white baseball boots. He reminded me of Timmy Mallet, the zany TV clown who liked to hit kids over the head with a rubber hammer.

'Alright, son,' my dad said as I opened the door. I looked at him bug-eyed but said nothing. 'Come on, then, we're going 'round your grandma's to cut the grass.'

I squished into the back of the van with the Irish Wolfhound, Riki, and his pregnant mum in her wellies. It was a short trip over to Grandma Joan's house and, as we pulled up onto her driveway, she was already standing outside. When my dad approached, she squinted at him for a moment as if she didn't recognize her son with his garish clothes and spikey blond hair. But my dad ignored her and he bent down to flip open the garage door.

'Go on and get the mower out, son,' he said as I peered into the musty outhouse. It was dark and there were cobwebs in there but, at the back, I could make out the shape of a bicycle. I ignored it and walked towards the orange Flymo. My dad followed close behind and pointed at the bike. 'It's yours.' His eyes crinkled in the corners as he smiled. 'We ain't gonna cut the bleedin' grass, are we?'

I stared at the bike, pie-eyed. 'Wait, wait...wha...?' I spluttered, flabbergasted.

'Yeah, well'—my dad stared down at his oversized baseball boots—'since neither me nor your mum could afford to replace your stolen bike, the old girl's gone and got you one out of her pension, ain't she.'

I wanted to say something good but all that came out was, 'Wha...? Woah!'

Grandma seemed as giddy as a schoolgirl with excitement. I was thrilled. It was a 12-speed Townsend Mango Creek. The thing was hideous: radioactive pink and luminous green; the colour of one of my mum's rhubarbs. But I loved it and I rode it everywhere. This time, I made sure to lock the bike up every time I got off it. And, of course, I used it to visit Grandma as often as I could.

Grandma Joan deteriorated in the years after her husband died. I regularly cycled over to hers and we'd fetch fish and chips. We talked and we watched *Blockbusters* together. She wasn't a sweet old lady—she was cantankerous and had bad habits—but I loved her, even if I never said it. One time, I was standing in line at the supermarket cigarette kiosk with her when an older gentleman in front of us turned to her and said, 'Filthy habit, isn't it, smoking?!' He shook his head and tutted in friendly disapproval. 'We should all give up really, eh?'

The poor man must have felt instant regret when Grandma became infuriated and hit him with a fierce diatribe: 'I don't care if you're eighty years old,' exploded the old woman, wagging a yellow finger in his frightened face. 'I might be only five and a half feet in my stockings, but nobody tells me what to do!' She might as well have kicked him in the bollocks with each syllable and then slapped him across the mouth with her heavy handbag.

In her final years, Grandma's health declined rapidly and she became known as the eccentric old bat in the neighbourhood. Nothing seemed good to her, except for crossword puzzles. When her neighbours enquired about my dad, her only son, Grandma told them that she hated him and wished he wasn't born. Her body was riddled with disease, she developed septicaemia and had to have her right leg amputated. It's like the old girl was sitting in death's waiting room, filling up her bumper crossword books until her number was called so she could go and join her husband.

'I wish the good Lord would come and take me,' she'd often growled in her low smoky timbre.

Grandma Joan died a few years later and, on the day of her funeral, I fucked up and went to the wrong place. Idiot! I ended up missing the service.

June 2020

After learning the date of Daryl's death, I get back in my car and quickly pull out of the crematorium to make the ten-minute journey over to the Luton library. I'm there in seven but a nervous young girl with glasses informs me that they are still closed to the public. I'll have to come back. I feel deflated, so I amble across St Georges Square and purchase chicken and chips from the same place where I'd met Leon a few months back. I sit on a low wall next to a couple of al-fresco drinkers and eat from the soggy cardboard box. It's not as good as last time, so I discard my food in a bin and decide to visit the streets where I grew up. Perhaps I think I'll find Daryl there. I drive calmly over to Pirton Road and park up just around the corner. As I pull up, I see a smackhead in my rear-view mirror. He's bowling down the road, limping, but shifting with real pace and purpose. Funny how you see these ghouls and goblins, purposefully speed-walking all around town, often early in the morning, as though they're running late for work or something. I sense the familiar adrenal sensation as my fight-or-flight kicks up a notch and I decide to wait until he's passed before I step out of my brand-new Volvo. My window is down and I can hear him talking to himself: 'They can't do me dirty like that. You get me?' the fiend mutters as he fucks off down the street, dragging his gimpy leg.

I catch a glimpse of the guy's scrunched-up face as he limps past. He's probably about my age, though it's hard to tell: he's got his hood up and the years of substance abuse seem to have taken their toll on his body. Could he be one of my old schoolmates?

I get out and stroll past where Karl the Old Station lived. The garages that used to be here have long been demolished and a neat cul-de-sac of red brick houses stands in their place. The old houses along the street are the same, except some of them now have double glazing. It's a warm day but the street is dead silent. No engines revving, no dogs barking, no shrieks of children playing, and no neighbours on their doorsteps, chatting and sharing mugs of tea. Probably all indoors, staring at their screens.

I walk down to what used to be the rough end of Pirton Road and arrive outside our old house. The same curved sixties-type numbers are hanging on the wall. I have a vision of the old photograph I found: the one where my mum is holding me in front of the house and she's got a fag and a feathered perm, and I'm wearing the green cardigan with trains on it. We're both smiling.

I reach down and touch the warm, cracked pavement where a dead kid once drew with a piece of petrified dog scat. A wave of emotion rushes up, so I suck it back in. I think about knocking on the door but I notice a sign in the net curtains that says 'Beware of the Rottweilers' and I change my mind. Instead, I stand there for a couple of minutes in the ghostly silence. I look over at the spot where Little Daryl got run over; there are now speed bumps there. I go around the corner, past the river and the bushes where I once did a poo. The area is still littered with cans and crisp packets. Around the back of the house, I try to snatch a peek at my old garden but it's completely overgrown. I cross back along the adjoining road and pass number 181. My brain pulls up a memory of a story about a guy who was shot and killed at that house. I remember when it happened; I must have been around eight or nine. Apparently, someone knocked on his door in the middle of the night, and as the resident leaned out of the window to see who it was, that someone shot him in the face. Everyone said it had been a case of mistaken identity. I make a mental note to look it up when I return to the library. I remember as a kid seeing the little pockmarks peppered on the brick around the window that looked like a constellation or one of those dot-to-dot pictures. Everyone had said that they were the marks left by the spray of the shotgun pellets. I'm surprised to see that they're still here. I wonder if the man's family still lives here or if the present occupiers of the house know about its history.

I instinctively navigate my way through these streets I know, gliding past the colourless walls and windows. I cross over to a scrubby patch of grass where an old TV, a mattress, and someone's jacket have been casually fly-tipped. I take out my phone and snap a couple of pictures for posterity. And at last, I tread over and stop directly outside what used to be Hookers Court. The street no longer bears the name Hookers Way and all the house numbers are different. Another example of people trying to gloss over the past? Or maybe someone's taken genuine initiative to try to polish up the image of the neighbourhood. If so, it hasn't worked; there's still pigeon shit and crap graffiti splattered around. A miserable-looking elderly couple is hobbling to get outside, struggling with the weight of the building's cell-like door. I nod and say hello. I think about venturing inside but decide not to. There are toys on one of the dusty balconies; evidence of children living here. A Luton Town flag hangs limply in one of the windows; others are boarded up with sheet metal.

I circle back to where the Man on Wheels pub once stood and past Barley Lane. It looks nicer now. Most of the well-known families like the Nashes, the Gadds and the Fosters have long since moved away. I take one last look around as an aeroplane knifes its way silently across the pale sky, then I get back in my car. There's nothing much to see here and as the engine launches into a low growl, a wave of apathy sweeps over me. Any urgency I may have had about visiting the library and following up on Little Daryl's story suddenly seems futile. The kid's gone; washed, dried, and put away, out of sight.

I flip the gearstick up and grip the steering wheel firmly as I tell myself to liven the fuck up and get with the programme. My journey will never be complete without it.

Part 3

The Truth

Chapter 16
Life Beyond Luton

Let me get this straight. You're married to a good-looking doctor who adores you, you live in the suburbs, you plan to build a garage, your new coupe is the envy of the neighbourhood, you're baking cookies in a gas-operated Magic Chef, and you're depressed?

Leslie Manning

My auntie Tracie and her husband Darren lived in one of the new suburban semi-detached houses with a doorbell and a driveway. They had met at a disco where Darren had worked as a disc jockey. Now, he ran a meatpacking business and owned a fleet of lorries which he used to transport his wares to markets all over the country. Darren and Tracie fascinated me because they went on holidays to Spain and brought back T-shirts and long strings of boiled sweets. They also owned an angular Toyota sports car which went like shit off a shovel. It had pop-up lights, electric windows, and a hologram sticker on the windscreen that said 'Darren & Tracie'. I buzzed with pride when Uncle Darren came to pick me up in his flash motor and took me to work on the various market stalls that he operated. Darren was big and loud, your typical Jack the Lad market trader. But a real grafter who showed the meaning of true hard work and what it could achieve. I don't think I helped Darren very much, though—my arms were too puny to lug heavy crates and scrub the walls of the massive meat chillers—but he paid me anyway, perhaps just out of kindness.

When I wasn't at work or exploring the neighbourhood on my bike, daring myself to go a bit further afield every time, I spent hours in my bedroom with the curtains drawn, pressing play and record on the Alba tape deck that my dad had got me. Bryan Adams had been at number one for weeks and a pair of dads were singing this dumb song called 'The Stonk'. Me, Leon, and Jit had performed a ridiculous dance to it at the end-of-school concert. But I wasn't into any of that New Kids, stonk, pop, acid house shit. I already knew what was cool. Instead, I would listen to the radio, patiently waiting for the likes of Salt-N-Pepa, Bobby Brown, or Janet Jackson to come on. The snappy drumbeats of American hip-hop, soul, and new jack swing echoed off my bedroom walls as I fantasized about a different life. A better, more varied life. A life beyond Luton.

With the money I earned at the markets, I could take the thirty-minute bus trip into town, having first sprayed myself all over with deodorant and pasted my hair back with a pawful of fluorescent gel, of course. Sometimes, it would be just me and Leon; other times, we rolled with a whole posse consisting of Marlon Foster, Keith Nash, and a quiet black boy named Roland who lived on my street. Roland's mum drove a puss-coloured Reliant Robin and, occasionally, to his embarrassment, she'd offer us a lift. But we always declined. We preferred to ride on the top deck of the number five bus. We weren't yet cool enough to ride at the back, so we always sat in the very front seats. It was good because there was a hole where we could stare down on the driver's bald patch and wind him up. We pushed our noses up against the sweaty glass as the bus weaved its way past the decaying Victorian terraces and pebble-dashed prefabs. Then, in stark contrast, it'd take us through the lively streets of Bury Park, which could have resembled downtown Karachi or Rawalpindi with its exotic sweet centres, halal butchers, and open boxes piled high with watermelons and sweet potatoes. From our moving perch, we played our own distasteful version of *Where's Wally?*—a humourless game called 'Spot the White Man'.

In town, we might wander through the Arndale and look at the hi-fis in Tandy's or buy a tape from Our Price, which we'd record on and then return the following week. Sometimes, we saw a movie, and we *always* used the coupon on the back of the bus ticket to buy a Big Mac for a pound. We'd sit on the curved stone steps in front of the ABC

Cinema and eat our slippery hamburgers while talking about who we were going to beat up and which girls we were going to nail when we started high school. Just as all eleven-year-old boys do, we thought we were the baddest dudes on the block.

The real bad dudes were some towering older guys who lurked in the arcade by the entrance of McDonald's. They would wait around there for unsuspecting kids like us to come along so they could relieve them of their pocket money. They would slide up close to us and rattle and jab our waists to hear if we had any loose change jangling in our pockets. And if they were feeling particularly cruel or wanted to humiliate one of us in front of our friends, they'd make us dance. The black kids mostly got left alone and I'd been jacked too many times before, so I kept most of my money safely tucked away in my sock. But I knew to keep a few coins at hand to appease the bad dudes if they got mean.

Normally, after finishing our food, we'd resume our patrol of the town. But I remember one occasion when I had to head home early because my dad was coming to pick me up and take me to his new place for the weekend. He'd recently got a council exchange to a village out in the country and I was intrigued by this new and exotic land he now lived in. I wondered how it differed from where I lived.

(Of course, Dad was late picking me up.)

On the drive over to his new house, I peered out the back of the van at the country roads as we wound away from town, thinking about what village life could be like. Would it be safe to go around on my own? Or would there be other kids for me to hang out with?

I leaned onto my side and subtly pulled out a folded-up piece of paper from my back pocket. It was an MC Hammer poster which I'd torn out of my *Smash Hits* magazine. I was planning to show it to my dad later as a reminder that he'd promised buy me a ticket to the concert. After deciding it wasn't the right time, I popped it back in my pocket.

When we arrived at my dad's new house, it was getting dark, so I couldn't see much of the surroundings. But the air smelled different—sort of green and earthy—and you couldn't hear anything except for a few strange bird noises.

The inside of the house was a mess, with boxes and bits of furniture dumped haphazardly across the un-vacuumed carpet. But even though it was untidy, I was excited to be there because Dad always let me do what I wanted. I could stay up late and guzzle Coke or eat Sugar Puffs straight from the box. And my dad had an elaborate sound system with gigantic speakers. I'd ask him to put on the old Michael Jackson records so I could fling my limbs about, grab my crotch, and drag my feet backwards along the floor.

Later that evening, when my dad was sitting down with a spliff and watching the telly, he told me to go to the kitchen to fetch his cup of tea. 'And bring me that white envelope that's tucked behind the kettle.' I did, and he said, 'Go on, open it.'

I peeled back the paper to reveal a picture of MC Hammer in his baggy pants. Inside were two tickets to the concert at Wembley. He'd said he was going to get me tickets. And he did.

'Happy birthday, son.'

I was delighted and I curled up next to my dad on the sofa. I knew he'd be settling in for a long night in front of the telly and that, within a few hours, he'd be completely fried to the point that he'd just stare at the on-screen image of a girl with a toy clown that came on after the channels stopped airing their programmes. So, I took the opportunity to question him about the countryside village where he now lived.

'What's it like 'round here, then, Dad? Are they friendly? Do they talk different? D'you ever get any trouble?'

'No, son, it's quiet and the people are nice. Not like Luton. You can go wherever you like and no one'll bother you. And if we bring your bike, you can ride off and explore the fields and country lanes. What d'you think about that, son, eh?'

I considered for a moment all the freedom I could enjoy in such a place. 'But how comes it's so quiet and peaceful, though? Do they have a lot of police 'round here or something?'

He paused. 'Funny you should say that. Pigs did come visit me the other day.'

'Why?' I asked.

'Er, well, it was to do with me plants, you know...?'

I did know exactly what plants he meant, so my follow-up question sprung out like a pinball: 'Will you go to jail?'

My dad cracked a smile. 'No, son.'

He did.

July 2020

I wake up late. The house is a mess and I feel wobbly, so I make myself a coffee and sit down to write a few lines in my diary before I tackle the housework:

> Woke up feeling like someone's got my head in a vice and they're slowly cranking the handle. Tension in my head, face, and shoulders. Blocked nose. Fear, sadness, and anger within. Andrea is doing yoga, the kids are on their games, and I'm a worthless fuck who doesn't deserve a family.

As I look back over my childhood experiences, my uncontrollable urges, the fights, the times when I used to beat my head against the wall in frustration, I realize that I was never mischievous or a troublemaker. Just agitated...and angry. It has become evident to me now that the constant constriction in my tummy and the ever-present, rhythmically pounding sledgehammer of dread informing me that something terrible is about to happen were just physical manifestations of molten rage and heart-pumping fear.

I've become accustomed to these sensations. I've learned to suppress and control them and even channel them into writing. And by writing about the past—the places, the characters, the tragedies of kids like Little Daryl—I'm developing an understanding of the rage and fear.

But that doesn't make it all go away. It always returns, bubbling up in the form of tension and physical pain, irritability, and fatigue. Sour thoughts goad me, causing me to think the worst of people. I instigate arguments. I write detailed angry emails which I'll never send. I plot escape routes and I play out imaginary confrontations in my head. I've read the self-help books and tried all types of treatments, techniques, and practices, but the relief has always been short-lived. I think my key preserving factors are that I have a patient and calm wife who supports me and loves me unconditionally and two beautiful, energetic children who spark light and joy into my days.

I could try to give the story balance by describing my now comfortable life. Healthy, rich with family, love, culture, and education. I could catalogue my achievements. Waffle about social mobility, multicultural communities, dysfunctional societies, violence, squalor, and the romantic notion of the ghetto. I could wax philosophical about politics and statistics. Pump my fist in celebration of overcoming disadvantage, gaining fortitude, and surviving hardship. I could say all those things but this ain't no Charlie Bucket kind of story. I have violent fantasies.

I could be walking down the street and I'll think of kicking dogs or ripping the bags off the old biddies at the bus stop. I have disturbing dreams about dead children and, when I wake up, I am so close to bursting into tears that I want to curl into a ball on the floor. Often consumed by fury, I wrestle with feelings of self-loathing: *I'm a cunt and everyone knows it.*

The truth is, I don't feel any different now than when I was a kid. I have the appearance of a middle-aged man but, inside, I'm still the same insecure wise-ass who likes fart jokes and will do anything for a cheap laugh. I'm just taller now, with a patchy beard and more experiences inked into my psyche; experiences that have formed part of who I am, which is why they keep coming back to me. I'm still a little boy who's scared all the time and forced to be on his guard. Forced to build walls, toughen up, and search for a way out.

It doesn't always have to be this way, though. Because I've learned that by understanding the past, I can find a way to rewrite the future. But before I can begin, I need to understand how one is supposed to be friends with themselves if they think the rest of the world despises them for who they are.

How can someone aspire to succeed if they're taught that status is determined by what shoes you wear and who you can have in a fight?

How can they build self-esteem if the image of oneself is that of a trashy little pleb with bad manners and dried bean juice down their trousers?

And how the hell could someone like Little Daryl possibly have survived when the odds were stacked so greatly against him?

And so, I suppose this isn't just about understanding what the past has done to others; I'm also beginning to understand what the past has done to me.

Chapter 17
Chaos and Kindness

Beware of the beige people.

Billy Connolly

As I entered my greasy teenage years, things began to get calmer. People stopped calling me Lossie and no one spoke about Little Daryl anymore. I tried to concentrate on my schoolwork and thoughts of the dead kid receded for a time. My lovely mum continued working hard, too. And she underwent a truly inspiring transformation: Zoe quit smoking, passed her driving test, and started university all in the same year. I still got into scrapes, and there are lots more stories to tell, but I faded more into the background. I drifted away—or perhaps, subconsciously, pulled away—from my old friends, knowing full well I'd never have friends like them again, aware that the times we shared were sometimes harsh and complicated but, at the same time, incredibly pure and simple.

And then, I got away. I went looking for new experiences after I left school. I attended college and university, worked many different jobs, and when I was left some money by Grandma Joan after she passed away, I used it to travel. Ever since I was a child, I'd wanted to know the world. I was once a page boy at my auntie Tracie's wedding and she gifted me a gold pendant featuring St Christopher carrying a child. I wore the gold medallion everywhere and although I ended up losing it, I never forgot about the patron saint of travellers. I wasn't allowed to use Grandma's money until I turned eighteen, so as soon as I could, I bought a one-way ticket and flew by myself to Los Angeles. It was late when I arrived at my downtown motel and I was startled to be awakened by a tattooed *mexicano* rattling at my door. At least I had the street sense not to let him in.

Despite the rocky start, I loved my time overseas, so I worked and saved more money to see different places. I went on adventures to Australia, Asia, and South America. I visited the islands of Fiji and thought they were a paradise. I was hooked and ready to see more. I called it 'the travel bug' but, really, I was just on the run from my life, from my roots, from myself. I disliked where I was from and wanted to be somewhere else. I'd reach far-flung, exotic destinations and feel great for a while until I realized that I was still me but in the sun. I learned a lot and collected lots of stories but parties, pretty girls, and beaches didn't fill the void inside. I still didn't know who I was or what I wanted. I read more self-help books to try and figure it all out. One was a book by Susan Jeffers called *Feel the Fear and Do It Anyway.* A line from the book which resonated with me was: 'If you always do what you've always done, you'll always get what you've always got.'

I took calculated risks. I learned to channel my nameless pain into resistance, hope, hunger, determination, and action. For me, thinking about my early struggles just made me want to push harder. Maybe I was just fortunate enough to have been born in a country with good infrastructure and a generous welfare state; a wealthy nation where education and healthcare are widely available and opportunities are abundant. Maybe I was blessed with a 'special sauce', whereby my unique genetic make-up is such that I'm resilient, allowing me to navigate life's hurdles, bounce back, and develop new skill sets. Maybe my brain can regulate its serotonin levels when they get too low, or is malleable enough to be pressed and moulded into different shapes. Maybe having children of my own gave me the drive to protect them from the types of things I had to face. Maybe, I don't know.

Truth be told, I think I just didn't want to become one of those people who spend their whole life in the town they grew up in. Staying in the same beige jobs for years and returning to the same beige places on holiday every summer. Chewing on the same piece of gum 'til it's dry and tasteless. Not that there's anything wrong with being contented but

I've just always felt that there is more, and the idea of living a life in beige filled me with dread.

It was on the island of Fiji that I met a girl called Renata. She was from Brazil. Small and pretty, with cascading black hair and a little turned-up nose which wrinkled when she laughed. We spent a whole week together, fooling around, exploring, and lazing on the beach. It was easily the happiest time of my life thus far. Renata was reaching the end of her trip and on her way back home. She told me all about her country and I don't know why but I experienced an instant connection with Renata and her homeland: they seemed to be the opposite of beige. I was drawn to the earthy warmth that she exuded and I was intrigued by the idea of the places I had seen on the maps—places with exotic names which she translated into things like 'Beautiful Horizon', 'River of January', and 'Sugarloaf Mountain'. Renata gave me a book by a Brazilian author called Paolo Coelho. It was a fable about a young boy called Santiago who goes on a journey across a desert to find his destiny. A particular passage stuck out: 'When you want something, all the universe conspires in helping you achieve it.'

When I got back home, I started thinking about my next trip straight away. I got out my map and was instinctively drawn to this little pointy bit at the top of Brazil which hooks out into the Atlantic Ocean. It was called Salvador. I'd never even heard of this city but the images of a lighthouse and the *bossa nova muzak* which looped over and over on the primitive website captivated me. It was at that moment that I realized it was possible to fall in love with a place. I knew I had to go there.

I took the train down to London and walked into a travel agency which specialized in trips to Brazil. I sat at a desk with a softly spoken man who sounded a bit like Speedy Gonzales. I explained where I wanted to go and his eyes lit up: the man said his name was Alfonso and that he was from Salvador. He tapped away at his keyboard and printed out the itineraries. We talked about the sights and possible things I could do there. I said goodbye, folded the papers into my jacket pocket, and stepped back out into the brisk air of London's West End.

When I returned a few weeks later to book the ticket, Alfonso explained that he had already made a phone call back home to his parents: 'Carlos, it will be mine big pleasure for you can stay with mine family when you going to Brazil.'

I was overcome with gratitude. Alfonso and I became friends; we ate a black bean stew called *feijoada* and he taught me my first words in Portuguese: *Quando você quer alguma coisa, todo o universo conspira para que você realize o seu desejo.* When you want something, the whole universe conspires to help you achieve it.

Sure enough, when I arrived in Salvador, Alfonso's brother was there waiting for me. André drove me across town to the house while drinking the stupidly cold *cerveja* straight from the beer can. The intense tropical heat was stifling—the white-hot sky baking the air into a thick gravy of sweat, coffee, trash, hot dogs, and sugary fruits—and the culture shock was like a hard punch in the face. The constant stimuli assaulted my senses: the colours, pastel stone walls, black-haired señoritas in bikinis, moss-covered paths zigzagging up into the favelas. And all of it set to a raucous orchestra of clanging, whistling, yelling, motors, and radios pumping strange and seductive music into my jetlagged ears. I breathed it all in, ate it up, absorbed it through my paper-white skin.

At the family home, they sat me in a reclining chair next to a fan and showed me music videos of a local band called Calcinha Preta (black thong) while the mother returned intermittently to brush my hair and hand-feed me chunks of watermelon. Once I'd got over the initial bout of sunburn and diarrhoea (a rite of passage for any gringo in the tropics), I settled in well. I ended up spending six weeks there, immersing myself in the language and the music and soaking up the local culture. It occurred to me while I was there that I could have visited anywhere in the world—wild Siberian deserts, rugged Alaskan peaks, or futuristic Asian cities—but, somehow, I felt right at home in the tropical jungles of Latin America. I easily navigated my way along the uneven streets in my Havana flip-flops, admiring the modern street art on the sides of leaning, decaying buildings, half covered by rags of posters. Tangled masses of electric cables dangled overhead and elderly amputees begged at the lights, grinning madly as if they hadn't a care in the world. The roads were thick with buses and carts, horns beeping and bells clanging, and dogs, bicycles, and wily kids selling sodas and peanuts weaved amongst the traffic. I soaked it all up and continued about my business as if it were all completely familiar to me. Maybe I was comfortable in South America because my status was automatically elevated on arrival. Where I'm from, I'm a nobody, but in Brazil, I was seen as interesting or exotic. Or perhaps I found my rhythm amongst all the chaos and kindness because, somehow, it reminded me of where I was from.

I returned home and immediately sent off for a pack of Portuguese audio CDs to listen to while picking the sand out of my belly button. I studied the beautiful language and the music. And I attended Latino events, which was how I met my Colombian wife, Andrea. We found a place together in London—the city that had fascinated me as a child—and enjoyed all the wonders that the capital has to offer. And then, one year later, our son was born and we bought a flat. That was the year I became an adult; when shit got real.

I think becoming a parent was probably what kicked all the memories and self-reflection into high gear: The immense pressure I felt to do it right or, at least, the opposite of the 'Emrys method'. The overwhelming sense of responsibility and breadwinning and sustaining a human life other than my own. The realization that life is mostly about taking the bins out, washing up, and doing laundry. The notion of impermanence you feel when you're young and single is removed from all that. You walk to a different beat.

We returned to Brazil for a family holiday last year but it wasn't how I remembered it. That's how it goes: things are never as good as your recollections, perhaps because you look back on youth with the sense of romance that is attached to those memories. Memories are, by their nature, random flashes which are frozen and neatly gift-wrapped, conveniently packaged into whatever we want them to be. Reality is different.

Becoming parents in our twenties hit us like a steam train and raising a family has been a slog, but we've coped. I think Andrea and I have been doing an okay job so far. Our children are now the age that I was in this story; their eyes bulge and shine when I tell them of some of the things I got up to when I was a kid; some of it they would never imagine doing.

It is early evening as I sit here and write this. I can hear my kids rustling around, talking and playing peacefully in their bedrooms. It gives me an enormous sense of comfort to know that they are healthy and happy, without fear of being robbed or run over...or of going to bed and not waking up.

After all this, my early years seem like another lifetime. A lot of things happened that were out of my control. But even at the time, I had a vague sense that the trajectory I was on was not the same as many other kids of my age. In the chaos of it all, it seemed like things were racing by at a hundred miles per hour and that my life was somehow different, not conventional, not exactly normal. But then again, nothing is normal when you're a kid; everything is exaggerated, time is distorted, and all adults are old and boring. But the past isn't another lifetime. Regardless of what we might think or want, it won't just go away or fade into the distance. It is in us; it's part of us. And if we truly want to deal with the monsters that dwell in the murky recesses of our minds, we must confront them sooner or later.

Chapter 18
The Dead Will Have Their Say

And many of those that sleep in the dust of the earth shall awake, some to everlasting life, and some to shame and everlasting contempt.

Daniel 12:2 (KJ21)

October 2020

The country has entered another lockdown and my mood is flat. I feel frustrated that everything is closed again. Now that I have Little Daryl's date of death, I could have gone to the town hall and applied for a death certificate or something. Heck, I could have walked into the library at any point over the previous months. Why didn't I?

I have no option but to dig around online again but all my searches are thwarted by a lack of information. I try all the usual lines of enquiry, online resources, and old-fashioned detective work. I even apply to the criminal justice archives but to no avail. There seems to be absolutely nothing out there. Unlike all the other stories of dead kids you see on the news, Daryl's picture and his name have somehow been erased, forgotten. But not to me, he isn't. He can't be forgotten because he departed at a time when I was just starting to form ideas about the world. But those ideas were fragile and the seismic thing that happened to him tore my undeveloped world apart. It showed me that death could come to anyone at any time. It taught me to be fearful of my surroundings because death might come to me. Little Daryl's death was where it all started for me, so I can't allow him to be just some other lost council estate kid. I won't leave him tucked away like some grimy piece of artwork confined to a vault, waiting to be restored. I was doing that, it's true. I realize that now. For years, I *had* shoved him to the back of my mind to deal with later. But later is now. I feel I owe it to him to tell his story. I owe it to myself, as well. It's time to stop hiding from the truth. I need to do what's necessary to find the facts.

I call the library but it's still closed, so I get in touch with a police officer friend who suggests I contact the county archives to see if they can provide any information. With perhaps a little more hope than I've had in a while, I fire off an email.

Less than a week later, I wake up at 8 a.m. and stretch my arm out towards my phone. I've developed a habit of checking my messages as soon as I arise. I think seeing the fresh correspondence gives me a hit of validation—confirmation that I'm loved and important—even if it's spam. I open my email and scroll down through the messages, assertively flicking my finger to swat the latest notifications into the delete folder.

'Buy Bitcoin'—(swat)—'Improve your Google ranking'—(swat)—'Black Friday deals'—(swat)—'Increase your manhood'—(Err, swat).

And then, there it is, buried amongst the junk: an email from the coroner's service. I hesitate to open it; I need to look at it on my computer screen. My heart beats a little faster as I get out of bed and snatch the bag containing my laptop. I flip open the screen and discover that the battery's flat. 'Shit.' I fumble as I quickly untangle the cable and plug in the MacBook. I type in the password as I sit on the edge of the bed in my pants.

My right hand twitches over the mouse pad: 'Dear Mr Meek. Thank you for your enquiry. We have searched our archives and have found the information attached. Please note that you may find the information distressing.'

I click on the attachment without hesitation and my eyes flick across the handwritten police report. There's a series of boxes containing names and dates and, at the bottom, a section containing the words: 'The death of a child was recorded at 02.30 hrs on Saturday 3 January 1987 at Hookers Way.'

I click through the pages that follow. They contain the coroner's and forensic reports which I scan carefully, trying to pick out the details that can help me build an image of the events.

It's apparent that the initial call came over the police radio and two uniformed officers attended upon the report of a body at the address. Once they had sealed off the area with yellow tape to preserve the scene, they immediately informed the Criminal Investigation Department (CID) who appointed a senior investigating officer to the case. The officers then summoned medical examiner Dr Peters, whose job it was to identify the body and pronounce the child dead legally. At 4.30 a.m., a further call was made to request that PC487 Alan Jones attend the scene on behalf of HM coroner. He arrived an hour later, along with the SOCOs (scene of crime officers) DC 'Ali' Hopkins and Tom 'Mick' Madigan.

I shuffle myself up the bed until I can rest my back against the wall, the laptop balanced precariously on my clenched knees. My mouth is dry and my breathing is irregular as I anticipate what might be on the remaining pages. The statements describe what the police saw in detail:

> I attended the scene on the discovery of a body at 43 Hookers Way, Luton, where I saw a child lying in bed.

> Rigor mortis was well established. The body was cold to the touch.
>
> The pillow was over his face. He had a yellow blanket on his trunk. He was wearing a blue T-shirt and blue underpants. The T-shirt was grossly bloodstained, mainly to the right side. There was blood smearing over both hands, more so on the right. There was also smearing on the right upper thigh at the front and, also, on the right buttock.

Upon removal of the pillow, it was immediately evident to the officers that the child's death had been caused by the gaping incised wound which ran across the side and front of the neck. There was a cut on the bedding next to the boy's head, as well.

Once the identification and certification processes were out of the way, the formal police investigation could begin. It was determined by Detective Chief Superintendent (DCS) Selwyn Davies that the death had occurred under suspicious circumstances. They were dealing with a major crime scene, so an incident room was set up and a briefing held. There, the DCS assembled a local task force of investigators who would be part of the enquiry until it was solved. Family liaison officers were dispatched, also, and a full forensic investigation would be launched. The head of CID, Mick Brown, was tasked with making an early morning call to the Forensic Department at the London University Medical

College. Dr Peter Vanezis was on call. He was an experienced scientist who had already worked on a number of high-profile inquiries and was on his way to becoming one of the country's leading experts in forensic pathology.

***

Icy rain sliced through the air on that January morning as Dr Vanezis turned off his headlights and stepped out onto the glistening kerb, dragging his camel-coloured overcoat over his wide, slightly hunched back. He greeted the two bobbies who were guarding the outer cordon before making his way through the threshold, dabbing his nose with a handkerchief and looking back at the police vehicles blocking both ends of the street. At 7 a.m., the sun wasn't quite up and the blue lights were bouncing off the walls of the flats. He was led into the building and escorted straight up to the child's bedroom where he cast his trained eye around the sparse space, taking in the Superman quilt and the few bits of rickety furniture. It was here that he silently set about conducting his preliminary examination of the corpse.

The two SOCOs, Hopkins and Madigan, had finished securing their evidence—taking photographs and putting various exhibits into brown paper bags—while Dr Vanezis meticulously took down notes which would later form part of his own specialized report. The pathologist worked swiftly and diligently, carrying out his usual tests on the body, taking out instruments from his black case and carefully replacing them.

It took Dr Vanezis less than thirty minutes to complete his on-site examination. He was responsible for covering a huge area of Southeast England, so was keen to push on with the invasive post-mortem and make his return journey to London. Despite his unconventional role and hectic workload, Peter Vanezis was a good-humoured man who he stopped to chat while removing his gloves and gown. He told the female detective sergeant (DS) who was involved in the inquiry that he preferred never to attend crime scenes unless it was absolutely necessary. He also remarked to the DS that this was a particularly unusual case and, due to the nature of the injuries sustained by the boy, this was one of the worst scenes involving a child that he'd attended.

However, he would later state in his report that apart from the mutilated remains of a seven-year-old boy lying in a crouched position on the single bed, there had been nothing else remarkable or untoward about the interior of the flat. There was no sign of any disturbance or a struggle; it looked like just an ordinary humble domestic set-up. The most crucial of the immediate pieces of information that Dr Vanezis was able to determine from his examination was that the bed was neatly made and the body appeared to have remained in the same position, undisturbed, for several days.

By 9 a.m. on the Saturday morning, the child's cadaver had been transported by private ambulance to the Luton and Dunstable mortuary where Dr Vanezis began his examination. The procedure took several hours. It was noted, among other things, that there were no defence wounds or other injuries and no physical signs of abuse. The scything injury across the boy's neck appeared to have been delivered in one fell swoop and trailed to the front of his face like a gory smile. The incision was much deeper on the left side, where the jugular vein and carotid artery had been severed. While a torrent of blood had gushed through the boy's brain and lungs because of the catastrophic cut, all other parts of his body were noted as being normal and healthy.

***

The post-mortem results also describe the boy as having bitten fingernails and grazed knees and as being well-fed. That is exactly how I remember him: just a normal knockabout neighbourhood kid. The second to last page of the report shows that a coroner's inquest was ordered and the cause of death was subsequently recorded on the death certificate as 'an air embolism and severe haemorrhage caused by a cut-throat wound'.

The final document is a single-page supplementary report which shows that some six weeks later, on 19 February, Dr Vanezis was called to attend the coroner's court where he met with the same female detective who had been at the scene. She showed him an item which had been recovered from a separate location to the flat. The piece of evidence was recorded on the paperwork as 'Exhibit AH/17: A sharp butcher's knife'. The steel blade measured twelve inches long and was five centimetres thick. Dr Vanezis was asked to look at the knife to ascertain whether he felt that it could have been the instrument that caused the fatal injury on the boy's neck. The forensic pathologist concurred that it most likely was, that it must have been brought down with force by an adult, and that this could have taken place while the child was awake or asleep. Since there was no sign of a struggle, he commented that it was likely that the child had been attacked and killed swiftly.

I like to think Daryl died this way: quickly, in his sleep, and without prolonged pain or suffering. But those two words: butcher, knife. Seeing them together, clinically recorded on the coroner's report, triggers something. The words snag in my brain and summon up a memory of what I'd heard on the news all those years ago. But it's not really a memory. It's more of a feeling: one of fear; sharp, fresh, animal-like fear. As a child, I'd heard those words in connection with Little Daryl's death and I'd felt tingly and afraid. I don't think I knew what they meant at the time, so I guess I must have buried them away in my subconscious: somewhere in a dark nook in my head, along with the memory of seeing the grave.

I adjust my position on the bed and flip back to the first page to reread everything all over again. It's going to take some time for all this information to sink in.

***

A few more months pass and, eventually, I receive a notification to say that the library has reopened. So, on Monday morning, I drive towards Luton. By now, I can feel a prodding turbulence deep within me, as if the sense of wanting to find out what actually happened is becoming stronger.

On the upper floor of Luton library, there's a huge aerial photograph of the town which covers a whole wall. It's been there for as long as I can remember, so it must have been taken in individual sections by planes or something and then stitched together. The map fascinated me as a child. I'd always loved looking at maps as they offered a glimpse of faraway possibilities. When I was younger, I wasn't tall enough to see my part of town in the north of Luton but, now, I can step up close to run my finger down Pirton Road and what used to be Hookers Way. Then along Dead Man's Alley.

The slender, bearded bloke manning the reference section of the library is wearing a name badge that says Rodrigo and, judging by his accent and appearance, I suspect he might be Brazilian. Normally, I would spark up conversation and show off my Portuguese language skills but not this time: there are more pressing things on my mind. Besides, Rodrigo doesn't seem the chatty type. He directs me towards the archives and I hunker down at a large white table, surrounded by high shelves packed with books and the occasional rustle and sniff of people studying.

Armed with my new information, I decide to try some different angles. I begin by sifting through all the available resources with determined resolve. With all my paperwork spread out on the wide plastic table, I work like a TV supersleuth, painstakingly poring over the newspaper archives for clues, cross-referencing with online public records to fill in the blanks and draw connections. My perseverance pays off and, eventually, I start to uncover some pieces of information which I hope will provide answers as to *why* or *how* Little Daryl was murdered.

The very first piece I happen across is a front-page spread of *The Luton News,* dated 7 January 1987. The headline reads: 'ANGUISH OVER SECOND KILLING'. I crumple my face and look directly up at the suspended ceiling light. *Second killing?*

I go back to my newspaper article and read on, discovering that Little Daryl's murder was not the first to have taken place within the family. I'm shocked to read that less than four years prior to Daryl's death, his father had been killed by relatives, as well.

The criminal justice archives reveal that by 1983, Daryl's parents had been living together for six years at a house in Luton town centre. During the summer of that year, they had gone to visit family up north, along with his mother's father and brother, when an argument broke out in the car over who should pay for the petrol. On 15 July, they were all back in Luton and celebrating the recent birth of a baby in the family at their local, The Blacksmiths Arms. There had been some further disagreement at the pub and Daryl's father left with his wife, Daryl's mum. Shortly after they had arrived home, two men burst into the house and set about beating Daryl's dad with an iron bar and leather belts wrapped around their knuckles. Daryl's mum later testified at St Albans Crown Court how she had stood at the top of the stairs and watched her own father and brother bludgeon her husband to death.

The court transcripts note that Daryl's uncle and grandfather were each sentenced to seven years for manslaughter in March 1984. Several months later, Daryl and his mother relocated across town to our estate where she set up home with her new lover, an unemployed petty criminal with a frizzy thatch of dirty-blond hair and a shifty demeanour.

It is difficult to determine exactly what happened next but I continue to excavate, gathering the facts and assembling them to form the most likely sequence of events. I manage to obtain the contact details of some of the professionals who were involved in the case. I have no idea if they will talk to me, or if they are even still alive, but I return home and begin making some inquiries. I send out a couple of tentative emails and, over the next few days, I receive the responses which will help me fill in the blanks.

By the tail end of 1986, Daryl's uncle and grandfather had appealed their sentences and were released from prison after serving just two years. At this point, Daryl's mother and stepfather were both twenty-six years old and married with a two-year-old daughter. The young family, including Daryl, were living at Hookers Court and had spent Christmas of 1986 together at their home. Little Daryl was given a new bike for Christmas. But based on the family history and information I have gathered, it is fair to say that it wasn't an altogether stable home and that Little Daryl mostly got by with minimal parental guidance.

When he wasn't at school or knocking about the neighbourhood with us kids, the boy was often left in the care of his stepfather. The pair seemed to get on well but the stepfather was a devious man. He never worked and he had a local reputation as a shady character who liked to cheat and swindle his way around town. The stepdad ran his sneaky scams wherever he could, including over at The Cement Shed or the Man on Wheels pub where he carried out various cunning deceptions to obtain free drinks. His favourite ploy was to buy a round with a twenty-pound note from which he had torn off the corner. He would keep the corner of the note and then return later to pay for another round with a lower-denomination note. After buying the second round, he'd return to the bar again with the torn-off corner, claiming he'd paid with the twenty pounds and that he'd been given the wrong change.

Sometimes, he would take Little Daryl with him on his forays, like in the days preceding Christmas when the pair went along to the local chemist. The stepdad asked the girl behind the counter if she'd give him an empty pill bottle so he could play a practical joke on a friend. The bottle was handed over and he wrote the name of Daryl's uncle and the name of a medication on its label. The pair proceeded on to the doctor's surgery where the falsified bottle was produced, along with a request for a prescription for some strong sleeping tablets. The doctor wrote a prescription for thirty-two capsules of temazepam and the stepdad returned with Daryl to the pharmacy to collect his haul of illicit meds. Unknown to the little boy, his stepfather's reason for obtaining these drugs formed part of a terrible plot which he had been hatching.

It was a couple of weeks later, on New Year's Eve, when the stepdad began to put his plan into motion. The weather was exceptionally cold and I imagine that Little Daryl may have spent the evening curled up on the sofa with his mother, watching television. His stepdad was busy rustling around in the unkempt kitchen, quietly trying to break open the pills to extract their contents. He put some of the powder into the closest inconspicuous thing he could reach for: the baby's bottle, which had been lying amongst the crockery in the sink. The stepdad then topped it up with a small amount of milk from an open carton, gave it a shake, and took it into the living room. He told Little Daryl that it was the baby's leftover milk and asked his stepson to finish it.

It wasn't long before the boy started to become woozy, so he went up to his bedroom, took off his jeans, and put himself to bed. Daryl's mum also retired to bed shortly after at around 9.30 p.m., and it was at this point when her husband did something unusual. He brought her a cup of tea which he never did. She took a few sips but said it tasted strange and bitter. The conniving husband just told her to drink up and even added a spoonful of honey to sweeten it.

As no toxicology report was produced, it is unclear whether the dosage was enough to have been fatal, thus indicating whether the stepdad had intended to kill the boy via poisoning. Regardless, he waited patiently until everyone was fast asleep. Only once the household was silent did he retrieve the large knife from on top of his wardrobe and creep into the boy's bedroom to finish the job.

After slaying the child, the stepdad carefully cleaned up and set about staging the scene. He washed the knife and made the bed, flattening down the Superman duvet and placing the pillow over Little Daryl's head to conceal what he'd done and to try to make it look like the bed was unoccupied. Once everything was in place, he sat in the dark and calmly smoked a cigarette before slipping away into the frosty night to plant the murder weapon in the garden of his wife's brother. The same brother who was recently released from prison for the manslaughter of Daryl's dad.

The next morning, with the boy's body still concealed in the bed, the man woke his wife, who was complaining of a severe headache. He told her that her son had already got up and gone to his grandmother's house. From here, the stepdad would set about creating his alibi. He already had the bags packed and told his wife that they were travelling up north to visit some relatives. They could spend the time up there together with their daughter while Little Daryl stayed with his grandmother. It was during their journey up north that he casually mentioned to his wife that her brother had dropped by during the night while she was asleep.

The family arrived at their family's home that evening and spent the night but, by the next day, the stepdad was becoming jittery. He even took himself to A&E at the local hospital, claiming he was experiencing a panic attack. He returned later to the relatives' house where they were staying and his behaviour became increasingly erratic. On the evening of Friday 2 January, he was still reporting to be unwell and told the family that he was going to return to Luton—alone.

He arrived home late that same day and knocked on a neighbour's door. He told the neighbour that he'd just returned from a trip up north and that he'd found the child's body inside the flat. He said that he suspected that it was the work of the boy's uncle and asked if the neighbour would go with him to the police station to inform the authorities that they had seen the uncle leaving the block the previous night. At around midnight, the stepdad and neighbour entered Luton police station to give a report.

The stepdad stated that he'd arrived back home, entered the maisonette, and discovered the child in the single bed. In his initial statement, the stepdad claimed that he had no idea what had occurred since he had been away but that he suspected the boy's uncle.

By the following morning, the stepfather and uncle were being questioned and the police investigation was underway. Detectives worked quickly and thoroughly to gather evidence and interview witnesses.

A search of the uncle's home was undertaken and the police found the butcher's knife buried in his back garden. The remaining pills and baby's bottle were discovered close by, also, secreted behind a brick wall.

It was during the subsequent police interviews that the truth became apparent. The stepfather was produced from the cells looking dishevelled, giving off an aroma of stale sweat and cigarettes. He spoke willingly, but his accounts of what happened were inconsistent and each time the police offered new evidence, he backpedalled and altered his version of events. As his clumsily concocted story began to unravel, it became apparent to the detectives that he had cooked up an amateur plan to murder the child and pin it on the uncle. But the stepdad had failed to think it through properly. Under questioning, it became clear the uncle had not been involved. And the doctor's report from the hospital up north didn't tally with the stepdad's story of a panic attack. The evidence wasn't pointing in Daryl's stepdad's favour and there were holes in his account. When he realized this, the sly man shifted the blame from the uncle to the mother, now claiming he had concealed the weapon to cover for her. Eventually, under pressure from police questioning, the suspect blurted out the words, 'I did it... But it wasn't planned.'

He then admitted that he *had* created the mixture of Benzos and milk in the baby's bottle but that it had been intended for himself as he was contemplating suicide. He claimed to have left the deadly cocktail on the side while he was watching TV and then Daryl had come along and drunk it. But the sinister truth was that he'd specifically prepared it to sedate the boy so he could easily and silently slash his tiny throat.

Chapter 19
Jay's Story

Understanding our past helps us rewrite our future.

Unknown

I put on a suit and return to Luton to attend a wake. It's the funeral of an old family friend of the Finnegans. And even though I haven't seen any of them for many years, I was pleased to be invited and want to pay my respects. Besides, it's good to get out and socialize.

The event is being held at a nondescript pub on the outskirts of town. A couple of Christmas decorations still cling to the walls and the place has got that typical pub smell: a mixture of stale booze, vomit, and those pineapple-chunk urinal cubes. Despite the smell, there's a jolly energy in the room.

A handful of serious drinkers are lined along the bar. Of course, Martin is there, and his brother Barry, but they're not as impressive as they seemed when I was a kid. They're both toothless old men now, their kind faces haggard and pitted from a lifetime of misuse. I'm surprised they're still alive, to be honest. They speak with love and affection for their friend and I think about how people only ever say nice things about the dead. And then I think about how it's probably important to see the good in all people, dead and alive.

The Finnegans are good people and they're all gummy smiles, thankful I've made the effort to come along. We talk a bit about the old times and some of the characters who have come and gone. I learn that Earl passed away just a few months prior: 'He'd got the cancer.' It had ravaged his whole body and, only a few short weeks after the diagnosis, he was dead. No one says anything nice about him.

Fat Davey is there, too. He's still fat but his physical stature has withered. I stand by the door and watch him for a while as he plays pool. Fat Davey is clearly inebriated but he's playing with the sharp focus and calculation of one of those dicky-bow-wearing boy-wonders off the telly. I notice how the drunk pensioner steadies himself on the bar between shots and, when it's his turn, he sets his pint down and swaggers around the table, folding his body clean in half like a balloon animal. He sights along the stick before sharply poking the balls so they run across the green cloth and into the pockets with tight accuracy and precision.

It doesn't take long for him to win his game and as I pass him on my way to the bar, Fat Davey turns and looks directly at me. I'm about a foot and a half taller than him as I stand there with my hands on my hips, peering into his glassy eyes. We face off for a couple of seconds like a pair of gunslinging cowboys meeting in a Wild West saloon.

'Alright,' I say, smiling. He cocks his fat head to one side like a pet awaiting a treat. 'D'you know who I am?'

''Course I do,' Fat Davey replies, holding out a scabby hand for me to shake. He doesn't—the knitting of his brow gives it away—but he's done his best to style it out. I'm not hurt or even surprised. The gear and booze have long since pickled his brain to such an extent that he probably doesn't even recognize himself.

More and more people arrive and the place is livening up. The Irish know how to throw a wake and Martin's mate had been putting money aside for years for this very occasion. There's a decent buffet of Caribbean food, too, laid on by the people who own the pub.

I can't help but keep turning my attention back to Fat Davey and later, while I'm tucking into a piece of jerk chicken, I notice he's fallen fast asleep on a chair over in a corner by the toilets. His sunken face is buried in his arms which are folded across his paunch. I'm not the only one who seems compelled to look out for him. Throughout the evening, people have been checking on him and offering him bits of food. He looks like a ghost of a man, as fragile as a baby sparrow. But me and everyone else there knows that he's still Fat Daisy, who'd once had a fearsome reputation on our estate and beyond.

Everything is the same, and everything is somehow so very different. These larger-than-life characters from my childhood, who made me laugh and cry, who played with me and made me cower in the corner, are all just old, fragile men now. Time and experience have shifted the power from them to me and I'm no longer afraid of them. The people from my memories, I realize, don't exist anymore. I don't have to carry that fear around like I used to.

But while I'm standing alone at the bar, surrounded by laughs and friendly banter and people doing their best to ignore the stained carpets and the cheap decor, I'm feeling a bit nervous and guilty. I've come with an ulterior motive. I take out my phone and check the time. It's 2.50 p.m.

A week earlier, I received a text message from someone who claimed to have been closely involved with Little Daryl's case: 'Hello. My name is Jay and I lived in the maisonette above. I was sixteen at the time. I knew the family. Contact me as I would like to gain some closure on this traumatic event that occurred so close to me at such a young age.'

I did some digging and Jay checked out, so I responded with an invitation to meet, today at 3 p.m. I peer through the window and see a lone figure sitting outside the pub. *Could it be him?* The man has a swarthy complexion and he's wearing an olive-green bomber jacket. He's bent over a bench and talking on his phone, so I wait, and as soon as he's finished, I summon the nerve to step outside to approach him.

'Alright, mate. You Jay?'

The figure looks up at me. 'Yeah,' he says in a deep, gravelly voice, slipping a filter between his lips and pulling his baccy pouch out of his jacket pocket. He has the look of someone who's been around the block a few times but I can see that behind his greying beard, there's the slight suggestion of a smile.

'Good to meet you.' I say. 'Wasn't sure if you'd come.' I suddenly feel all wired with a sort of nervous energy and I realize that I need to do something to break the tension. I raise a finger in the air. 'Gimme one second.'

I dash back inside the pub to buy Jay a drink. It's a cold day but as I wait at the bar, I notice that I'm sweating like a rapist. I have no real idea who this Jay fella is or what he might say. I don't even know if he'll talk to me now.

I hand Jay his pint of beer, for which he's grateful, and I slide onto the wooden bench opposite him. To break the ice and sound him out, I ask him about the old neighbourhood: 'D'you remember the Man on Wheels pub?'

'Yeah, of course I do,' Jay chimes. 'Everyone used to drink in there.'

'And by any chance, did you happen to know a fella called Zaki?'

'Zak? Yeah, I knew Zak.' Jay's smile widens. 'I used to knock about with him. I knew everyone 'round there. Zak was a heavyweight boxer. He was good. And they offered him a contract at The Thomas A'Becket gym. That's when he moved to London, see. And we all went down there one time to visit him. But London's a bit different from Luton. It was all the drinking and nightlife what done it. He got into an argument in a pub. Apparently, the geezer had just come off a seven-stretch for manslaughter. He waited outside the pub for Zak to come out and he stabbed him. Dead.'

'Oh, right,' I say, trying to keep my voice steady. Jay is already on his second roll-up and he's reeling off more names of people from the area who have lived and died, but I'm still thinking about Zaki. I remember how my mum had told me that a lot of stuff went on on the estate. As if life was cheap and violence was normal. I'm saddened but not surprised about Zaki. To be honest, I'd suspected something like that was the case.

'And there's plenty more stories like that 'round there,' Jay says.

There's a lengthy silence and I see this as my chance to broach the subject. 'So, anyway, you wanted to talk about this kid, Daryl?'

His dark brown eyes meet mine and his chin drops to his chest. There's an even bigger silence and I wonder what he's gonna do next. Is he gonna get up and walk away? Burst into tears? Hit me?

He takes another drag and blows out a big ball of smoke before rubbing his pock-marked forehead with the palm of his hand. 'Yeah, well, them days was fuckin' donkeys years ago now. An' I've never really spoke about it, see. So, I s'pose it would be good to get it outta me head.'

'Did you know the family well?' I ask.

'I was like family with them. I stayed there the night before it all happened. I used to stay there all the time and Daryl's stepdad used to take me to football. You see, my mum was alcoholic and my dad weren't there, so he showed an interest in me. He even showed me the knife. He'd been and got it sharpened and would cut up bits of fabric and stuff to show me how sharp it was.

'And he hated Daryl's mum's brother 'cos of all what happened before. That's where he thought of a plan, see. Revenge, like. He had it all planned out. He's gone and got the sleeping tablets in her brother's name and, after killing the kid, he planted the knife in the brother's back garden.

'And the next morning, he was already up, bags packed, and tells his wife they're heading up north for a few days. Before they left, he even asked my mum to look after the cat. Gave me mum a key to the flat and she was supposed to go in and feed it. But like I said, she was an alcoholic, so she didn't bother. His plan was that my mum would find the body. But she didn't, like, so that's when he had to come back home a couple o' days later.' Jay's on his feet now, gesticulating and vigorously puffing on his rolly as he relays his account.

'Makes sense,' I say, trying to regulate my breathing. 'He was hoping someone would go in and find the body while he was away. But they didn't.'

'Exactly! So, he's come back late that night and up to my house when he tells me he's just got home and found the kid's body. I'd been on a night out and didn't believe him. I called my older brother into the room and he didn't believe it, neither. So he's gone, "Come on downstairs, then, and I'll show you. But if the police asks you anything, just say you seen her brother coming in here while I was away." That's when me, my brother, and the dog have all gone down with him to look at the body.

'We've got to the door and the dog wouldn't go in. It was hot inside because they've got the heating on but all the lights were off, so we've gone in there with a torch. And we've gone in and opened the bedroom door and that's when I've seen what I've seen. My brother just turned around and ran off. Left me there with him. I've looked up at him and he's looked at me. And he was a big, tall man, you know?! And I was only small. And we've both looked at each other and then I've just run out of there.

'I've gone up to my other brother's house and told them. But they didn't believe me, see, 'cos I was a little shit back then. But eventually, we've all gone home, back to my mum's house, told her what's happened, and then my mum's gone and got him in a taxi and took him up to the police station. They kept my mum in overnight because they didn't know if she was involved or not.'

I pause to think about how I'd felt as a little kid. The fear I'd felt, and I hadn't even known what had actually happened. But Jay had seen and experienced it all first-hand. It must have been so much more magnified for him.

'Fuck!' I say as I slowly exhale. 'That would've been really tough for you to deal with.'

'On seeing the body, I've just shit myself. I slept in me mum's room for about a year after that.'

'And do you remember anything else about after? What was the situation? Did you have to give an interview or anything?'

'After it all happened, there was loads of police around. But they never asked me nothing. Not even an acknowledgement. If something like that would have happened these days, you would have had counselling or something. But back then, nothing. That's why I didn't have to give a statement or go to court. I suppose my mum probably never told them I knew anything just to keep me out of it. I remember the bloke from the paper come 'round one day, knocking on the door and asking me questions. But me mum told them to fuck off, like.

'Then one day, they brought him back. Two meat wagons full of police and a couple of cars.'

'What, the geezer who did it?'

'Yeah. Must've been a few weeks after it all happened. They've got him handcuffed. Must've brought him back to the house to go through things. Reconstructions or whatever. They was in there for about an hour or so. I was on my balcony, looking down, and as they've brought him out the van, everyone in the flats started kicking off and shouting, "Kill him. Kill the fucking murderer." I remember all that. It took them nearly a year to go to court and get him convicted. Took them eight months just to remove the bloodstained mattress out of the flat. I saw it. It was all dried up and a dirty brown colour.'

'The other thing I wanted to ask you about was the grave. Did you go to Daryl's funeral?'

'Yeah, I went to the funeral. It was over at Marsh Farm. And he was buried at the Luton crematorium.'

'But the gravestone's gone,' I say. 'I've been up to the cemetery and there's no gravestone. Do you know why?'

'What no grave? There must've been.' There's a pause. 'Oh, yeah, I think maybe that's because it was only a little wooden cross. Family couldn't afford a gravestone, so it was just a little wooden cross with a picture on it. And that would've rotted away years ago.'

'Oh, that makes sense. And what about the family? Did you ever see them again?'

'Nah, they all moved away.'

'Do you reckon you'd talk to them again if you got the chance?'

'Yeah, I think I would,' Jay replies. 'All I'd want to know is why. Why the fuck did he do it?'

We've been chatting for ages, and Jay is shivering. I've got my big winter coat on with the collar turned up but he's only wearing his bomber jacket. His teeth are chattering like a skeleton on a ghost train, so I stand up and offer my hand. He grabs me with the firm grip of a manual labourer and pulls me in for a half-hug before slotting a fresh rollup behind his ear and disappearing through the pub's double doors. The puke-pineapple smell hits me again but I feel much lighter after having spoken to Jay and I hope he does, too.

I look up at the darkening sky as I cross the car park and start thinking about how no one can ever really know exactly why the stepdad did what he did. How somebody could have the capability to slaughter a sleeping child is obviously beyond my amateur skills. And without knowing where the stepdad is now, it's not like I can ask him. Anyway, I don't think I'd want to speak to him even if I could.

Still, perhaps there's one more thing I can do to bring Little Daryl's story to a conclusion.

Chapter 20
Justice for Little Daryl

> Death no longer has dominion over him.
>
> Romans 6:9 (KJ21)

I return to the library a week later and locate the official documents which stated that the stepdad was charged with murder at Luton Magistrates' Court on 30 March 1987. The day before Little Daryl was buried.

The trial began eight months later at St Albans Crown Court with Richard Gibbs leading the prosecution. The Queen's Counsel commissioned psychological examinations for the defendant which portrayed a profile of an intelligent and calculating individual who was of sound mind and acted with intent. There was a sombre mood inside the courthouse as the jury listened to the image portrayed of a hypochondriac with a skewed outlook on life—someone who invented stories and feigned illnesses for his personal gain, even when it was to his own family's detriment.

The prosecution put forward their forensic evidence and the coroner's findings, which stated that the impact of the knife had broken two bones in the boy's neck and had almost severed his head. Witness statements were read out, and Exhibit AH/17 was produced. The hushed court heard how the suspect had gone into the local butcher's shop a month before the killing and paid £11.50 for the two-foot-long blade, under the pretence that he needed it to carve his Christmas turkey. Another witness statement described how he had shown the knife to a neighbour, informing them that it was 'sharp enough to cut your head off'.

The police records revealed a history of petty crime and that the man in the dock had been awaiting a court appearance for theft when he carried out the murder. Evidence was put forward on the various scams he operated around town and how, in some of his schemes, he had used Little Daryl as a prop. The jury was told about how he would often take his stepchild into town and shoplift specific items such as ladies' clothing, then get the angel-faced boy to return the items, saying that he had purchased them for his mum's birthday. The prosecution described the accused not as a violent brute but as a scam artist and confidence trickster who devised elaborate plots to con people out of their money.

The general impression put forward by the prosecution was that the defendant had carefully laid out a false trail of clues, hoping the background of bad blood between his wife and her brother would make it look as though the boy's uncle had committed the murder. They cited his motivation as jealousy towards his wife, whom he believed loved the child more than him.

The accused sat limply in the dock until it was his turn to be called up to the wood-panelled witness box. Wearing black trousers and a loose-fitting white shirt, he shuffled towards the stand, escorted by a court officer. He was a tall man but he cut a frail and pitiful figure as his narrow eyes scanned the dreary, windowless courtroom, before quietly muttering the oath through stained teeth. It was apparent that he'd spent the last eleven months on remand while the prosecution built the robust case against him.

Since he had pleaded not guilty to murder, the defence solicitors assembled a case based on the grounds of diminished responsibility. They attempted to draw a measure of sympathy from the jury as they gave an account of how he had come from a broken home and had experienced a troubled youth, how his parents had separated when he was young, and while his siblings stayed with their mother, he'd been left in the care of his abusive father. A psychiatrist gave evidence that he was an immature adult who had settled into a cycle of criminal behaviour. A report was produced which referred to psychiatric issues such as anxiety and personality defects.

Under cross-examination, the defendant spoke softly, occasionally stumbling over his words as he admitted that he *had* purchased the knife and that he had used it on Christmas Day, even though forensic evidence revealed that it had been stashed away and remained unused until the night of the murder. He admitted to having planted the capsules and the knife in his brother-in-law's garden but denied trying to set anyone up for the murder. An evil aroma emanated from the dock as he broke down in tears and claimed that he had intended to kill himself that night, but the child had woken up, so he'd panicked and become dizzy. The stepfather stated that he couldn't account for what had happened next. He also denied drugging his wife. 'I never intended to hurt anybody that night,' he said through his sobs.

On 4 December 1987, the court assembled for the final time. Spectators were packed into a sweaty courtroom number 4 as the evidence was laid out and the case was summed up by the judge. After five and a half hours, the jury was ushered back inside and the foreman rose from the bench to announce that a majority verdict of ten to two had been reached. The jury was satisfied beyond all reasonable doubt that the murder had been planned and methodically orchestrated by a cold and cunning individual, who was premeditated in the committal of the vile and heinous act. He was sentenced to life in prison.

The public records and documentary evidence have helped to bring closure to Little Daryl's story, even if they don't go any way to express the true horror and helplessness caused by the loss of a child and the profound impact it must have had on the family. And while some may not realize it, the effects of such terrible events can ripple through time and space and touch people they've never even met, sometimes for many years after.

***

The pandemic has all but blown over and it feels like a thing of the past. Life has pretty much returned to normal and the weather's good. I have good and bad days but, for the past few weeks, I don't have the nightmares anymore. Rather, I've been having this recurring dream every time where I'm living in a big old house that has one secret room which has been sealed off. It's usually an attic or some mysterious chamber located down a dark passage, separate from the main house. I have a sense that there are strange and scary things in that room and I am afraid to go there. Usually, the dream ends as I'm peering through the cracks in the windows or thinking about heading along the passage towards the locked door. Sometimes, I hear strange noises or see things being thrown from the room and I wake up to what feels like a jack-in-a-box going off in my chest.

But then the time comes when I don't wake up. The dream continues and I arrive at the door which was crudely boarded up with old planks of wood. My son and daughter help me to pry open the door and we crawl through the gap. There's dirt and bits of trash strewn around inside the room and I can see a small figure standing in the middle of the derelict grey space. It's a young child of about two years. It looks hideous, resembling one of those demonic dolls from horror movies: dressed in filthy rags with dark recessed eyes, matted hair, and deep wounds and pits on its face. I feel afraid of the tiny monster.

But I enter the bare room and walk towards it anyway. My instinct is to attack the gruesome puppet but I resist, instead embracing my urge to pick it up. I hold out my arms and lift the creature up and, right before my eyes, it transforms into a clean, happy child, now smiling and free of all the muck and scars.

I put the baby into a carrycot and my son and daughter help me tidy the room so they can use it. The once dark, dirty room is now clean and bathed in light. The door we came through is no longer boarded up and now leads out to a terrace with a beautiful view. My two children wander outside. Before I follow them, I turn to look at the baby in the cot and I say, 'You'll be okay. You'll be okay.'

Afterword

When I started this journey, I wasn't sure why I felt so driven to find out what happened to Little Daryl. I think I wanted to bring the dead kid back to life so he could be remembered. But I wanted to understand myself, too. I wanted to figure out why I put up barriers, fought back, and became the bully to avoid being the victim. And I wanted to know why, no matter how far away from Luton I got, my demons kept on following me.

Some of the anxiety I experienced throughout this process came from the fear that learning the truth about mine and Daryl's past would only make things worse. I'd half expected that trudging up ancient history would tear me up. But I'm not devastated, and neither am I relieved or exhilarated. Instead, it feels like something more peaceful—like doing laps around the block and returning home. By forcing myself to confront the truth about what happened to Little Daryl and the truth about how it—and all the other things that went on on that estate—affected me, I no longer need to imagine what dark things might have happened. The fear is absolved.

Of course, dark things *did* happen, but the light of truth has been shined upon them. And so, I don't feel shock or grief or even sadness, really. Just a sense of calm and familiarity, as if I have always known. Like I'm part of Little Daryl's story because our lives entwined and overlapped. I followed the ripples out from his death to see how they impacted me and, now, I understand myself better because of it. I see, now, that his death was the start of all the fear I used to feel, and that it happened at such a crucial time in my own development, shaping so much of who I was to become as a man. And by understanding this, I am finally in a position to make my peace with it—and maybe, one day, even manage it.

Maybe some of my problems derive from survivor's guilt: a feeling of being undeserving of the life I had when Little Daryl never had a chance. Maybe a part of me wishes I could have done something to save him or feels that it should have been me. The cards were stacked against him. His narrative was needlessly curtailed, cut short by a blood-drenched butcher's knife. Little Daryl never went to Leagrave Junior School or got to go on family trips or experience excessive Christmases. He met his fate prematurely and never got to complete his story. To shine, love, study, travel, get married, have a family, live to feel the burden of work and expectations like I did.

But maybe it was supposed to be this way and our friendship means we have both been able to endure longer than we would have otherwise: the dead boy gets to live on through me, and telling his story is the key to helping me to get better. In a way, discovering the truth and sharing his story doesn't just bring him back to life; I've brought myself back to life, too.

I'm not going to lie—it wasn't a deep friendship. Had he survived, we probably wouldn't even be friends now. He was just a kid who lived down the street. Our paths merely crossed. But you remember your friends. I remember how we played together on the grimy pavement and sucked on sticks of rhubarb in the garden. But mostly, I remember how I had imagined all the blood and how I thought I was next.

I set out wanting answers to questions. And while I have some of those answers now, I've realized that what was more important was hauling myself through the labyrinth of memories, going over every detail and into every hidden corner with a flashlight, brushing away the cobwebs, exploring dark vaults, unpacking boxes, confronting truths, unravelling long twisted threads of events... By undertaking this journey and laying out all my findings on the table, I now view my youth differently. I've obtained a new perspective and reawakened memories of a varied and happy childhood. Sure, things were tough sometimes. But they were often joyful, too, and mostly normal. I had some good people around me who looked after me with kindness and warmth and affection—people who contributed in all different ways and taught me things without me even knowing. Important things, like cloud formations and river jumping and creative cursing and the fact that American wrestlers are morons. But they taught me values, also: hard work, determination, loyalty, and courage. They were people who clothed and fed me, kept me safe and happy, gave me love and comfort and shelter. People like my mum, my dad, Martin, and Little Daryl. And for that, I'm grateful. Maybe they were unconventional or even dysfunctional, but they cared. It's taken thirty years but this journey has helped me to see that, I was lucky.

ACKNOWLEDGEMENTS

Firstly, I wish to acknowledge those whose lives have been impacted by the story and the subject matter within this book. I ask for forgiveness for the intrusions, and I hope that some comfort may be found in my efforts to preserve the memory of 'Little Daryl' (alias used to protect the family's privacy).

I would like to express my gratitude to Marnie Summerfield Smith from Your Memoir, Jenny Todd from TLO, and Richard McColl from Fuller Vigil, for championing my work and for seeing the story's potential from day one. A huge thank you to The Open Book Editor, Dan Cross, for working your magic on the manuscript, and to Tim Barber of Dissect Designs for the fabulous book cover.

I am also grateful to TLC Free Reads, Jericho Writers, Paul Ashby, Fabbio Scarito, Isabella McMurray, Teresa Coburn, and Colin Post for reading my early drafts and providing invaluable feedback.

Thank you to my fellow writers—Kit de Waal, Katy Massey, Chris Dresser, Wendy Moore, Simon Booker, Duncan Campbell, John Hegley, and Alexis Keir—for your friendly words of encouragement and helpful advice.

To the Bedfordshire Archives, coroner service, and Luton and British libraries, as well as to Alwyn Oakley, Peter Vanezis, Pete Balmbro, and the Bedfordshire National Association of Retired Police Officers branch for their assistance in my research.

Most importantly, I would like to thank my wife, Andrea, and my children, Santiago and Gabriela, for their unwavering love and support. The same goes for my mum and dad, siblings, and all my family and friends. Finally, I would like to give a shout-out to the good people who make up the vibrant community of the place I am proud to call my hometown: Luton.

About the Author

Carl Meek was born and raised in Luton, UK, and has lived in various parts of the world—most recently in Colombia, South America. He has always enjoyed reading and writing, and describes his unique style as 'honest and unfiltered narrative non-fiction: real stories of real people, with investigative elements'. *We Were Seven* is his first book.

Printed in Dunstable, United Kingdom

74721950R00168